W9-BCZ-136

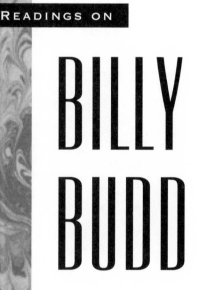

READINGS ON

BILLY BUDD

OTHER TITLES IN THE GREENHAVEN PRESS LITERARY COMPANION SERIES:

AMERICAN AUTHORS

Maya Angelou
Stephen Crane
Emily Dickinson
William Faulkner
F. Scott Fitzgerald
Robert Frost
Nathaniel Hawthorne
Ernest Hemingway
Arthur Miller
Flannery O'Connor
Eugene O'Neill
Edgar Allan Poe
John Steinbeck
Mark Twain
Walt Whitman
Thornton Wilder

AMERICAN LITERATURE

The Adventures of Huckleberry Finn
The Adventures of Tom Sawyer
All My Sons
Black Boy
The Call of the Wild
The Catcher in the Rye
The Crucible
Death of a Salesman
Ethan Frome
Fahrenheit 451
A Farewell to Arms
The Glass Menagerie
The Grapes of Wrath
The Great Gatsby
My Antonia
Native Son
Of Mice and Men
The Old Man and the Sea
One Flew Over the Cuckoo's Nest
Our Town
The Pearl
A Raisin in the Sun
The Red Pony
The Scarlet Letter
A Separate Peace
The Short Stories of Edgar Allan Poe
The Sun Also Rises
To Kill a Mockingbird
Twelve Angry Men
West Side Story

THE GREENHAVEN PRESS
Literary Companion
TO AMERICAN LITERATURE

BILLY BUDD

Laura Marvel, *Book Editor*

Daniel Leone, *President*
Bonnie Szumski, *Publisher*
Scott Barbour, *Managing Editor*

GREENHAVEN
PRESS®

THOMSON
━━━━✱━━━━™
GALE

San Diego • Detroit • New York • San Francisco • Cleveland
New Haven, Conn. • Waterville, Maine • London • Munich

For more information, contact
Greenhaven Press
27500 Drake Rd.
Farmington Hills, MI 48331-3535
Or you can visit our Internet site at http://www.gale.com

LIBRARY OF CONGRESS CATALOGING-IN-PUBLICATION DATA

Readings on Billy Budd / Laura Marvel, book editor.
   p. cm. — (The Greenhaven Press literary companion)
Includes bibliographical references and index.
ISBN 0-7377-0429-2 (pbk. : alk. paper) — ISBN 0-7377-0430-6 (lib. : alk. paper)
   1. Melville, Herman, 1819–1891. Billy Budd. 2. Sea stories, American—History
and criticism. 3. Executions and executioners in literature. 4. Impressment in
literature. 5. Sailors in literature. I. Title: Billy Budd. II. Marvel, Laura.
III. Greenhaven Press literary companion to American literature.
PS2384.B7 R43 2003
813'.3—dc21
                                   2002072573

"Truth uncompromisingly told will always have its ragged edges."

Chapter 28, *Billy Budd, Sailor*

CONTENTS

Chapter 1: The Plot and Characters of *Billy Budd*

Billy Budd, Sailor, evolved from a short prose introduction to the ballad "Billy in the Darbies." The manuscript reveals that Melville concentrated first on developing Billy's character, then moved to Billy's antagonist, John Claggart, and finally focused on the character of Captain Vere.

Several biblical references in *Billy Budd, Sailor* suggest that the work can be read as a Christian allegory; a retelling of the fall of man in the Garden of Eden. The work can also be read as both psychological allegory and secular allegory.

Claggart is specifically identified with the snake in Eden, but he may not simply be the personification of evil. Melville was fascinated by a sect of Gnostic Christians who venerated the snake as a source of wisdom in Eden, and he was aware that the snake is considered a symbol of eternal life in many Eastern religions.

Melville compares Captain Vere to the "Great Sailor" Lord Nelson and portrays Vere as a modest aristocrat, a well-read practical philosopher, and a statesman who acts prudently on his convictions for the good of the community. Captain Vere's aristocratic virtues are tested aboard ship.

Chapter 3: Themes in *Billy Budd*

Budd is clear: Public execution is not a deterrent; hanging as a method of execution is barbarous; and state execution of a person who kills accidentally, without preplanning or malicious intent, makes the state more guilty than the accidental killer.

FOREWORD

*"'Tis the good reader that
makes the good book."*

Ralph Waldo Emerson

The story's bare facts are simple: The captain, an old and scarred seafarer, walks with a peg leg made of whale ivory. He relentlessly drives his crew to hunt the world's oceans for the great white whale that crippled him. After a long search, the ship encounters the whale and a fierce battle ensues. Finally the captain drives his harpoon into the whale, but the harpoon line catches the captain about the neck and drags him to his death.

A simple story, a straightforward plot—yet, since the 1851 publication of Herman Melville's *Moby-Dick*, readers and critics have found many meanings in the struggle between Captain Ahab and the whale. To some, the novel is a cautionary tale that depicts how Ahab's obsession with revenge leads to his insanity and death. Others believe that the whale represents the unknowable secrets of the universe and that Ahab is a tragic hero who dares to challenge fate by attempting to discover this knowledge. Perhaps Melville intended Ahab as a criticism of Americans' tendency to become involved in well-intentioned but irrational causes. Or did Melville model Ahab after himself, letting his fictional character express his anger at what he perceived as a cruel and distant god?

Although literary critics disagree over the meaning of *Moby-Dick*, readers do not need to choose one particular interpretation in order to gain an understanding of Melville's novel. Instead, by examining various analyses, they can gain numerous insights into the issues that lie under the surface of the basic plot. Studying the writings of literary critics can also aid readers in making their own assessments of *Moby-Dick* and other literary works and in developing analytical thinking skills.

The Greenhaven Literary Companion Series was created with these goals in mind. Designed for young adults, this unique anthology series provides an engaging and comprehensive introduction to literary analysis and criticism. The essays included in the Literary Companion Series are chosen for their accessibility to a young adult audience and are expertly edited in consideration of both the reading and comprehension levels of this audience. In addition, each essay is introduced by a concise summation that presents the contributing writer's main themes and insights. Every anthology in the Literary Companion Series contains a varied selection of critical essays that cover a wide time span and express diverse views. Wherever possible, primary sources are represented through excerpts from authors' notebooks, letters, and journals and through contemporary criticism.

Each title in the Literary Companion Series pays careful consideration to the historical context of the particular author or literary work. In-depth biographies and detailed chronologies reveal important aspects of authors' lives and emphasize the historical events and social milieu that influenced their writings. To facilitate further research, every anthology includes primary and secondary source bibliographies of articles and/or books selected for their suitability for young adults. These engaging features make the Greenhaven Literary Companion Series ideal for introducing students to literary analysis in the classroom or as a library resource for young adults researching the world's great authors and literature.

Exceptional in its focus on young adults, the Greenhaven Literary Companion Series strives to present literary criticism in a compelling and accessible format. Every title in the series is intended to spark readers' interest in leading American and world authors, to help them broaden their understanding of literature, and to encourage them to formulate their own analyses of the literary works that they read. It is the editors' hope that young adult readers will find these anthologies to be true companions in their study of literature.

INTRODUCTION

When he died in 1891, Herman Melville left a heavily revised and disordered manuscript of *Billy Budd.* Thirty-three years later Raymond Weaver attempted the first transcription of Melville's handwritten pages, and in 1962 Harrison Hayford and Merton M. Sealts Jr. completed the now standard transcription of *Billy Budd, Sailor.* Although many scholars consider Melville's final novel unfinished, or at least not completely revised, Melville himself was not averse to a certain degree of incompletion and lack of formal perfection when attempting to embody elusive and intractable truths. In fact, Melville writes near the end of *Billy Budd, Sailor,* "Truth uncompromisingly told will always have its ragged edges."[1]

At its heart *Billy Budd, Sailor* is a painful and powerful exploration of one central incident, set aboard a British warship in 1797. This incident seems straightforward enough. A young sailor is falsely accused by his superior officer of fomenting mutiny. He responds to the false accusation with a blow, which kills his accuser. The only witness, the captain, understands the characters of both the sailor and the officer, yet he convenes a drumhead court and urges its members to sentence the sailor to death for killing a superior. They reluctantly do so, and the sailor is hanged, blessing the captain in his final words. Although this incident seems straightforward in outline, Melville designs his narrative in such a way that it provokes deep thought about the central characters and encourages multiple interpretations of them and the meaning of their words, actions, and decisions.

Parenthetically identifying his short novel as "an inside narrative," Melville invites readers to probe the inner motivations of his three central characters, yet at the same time creates a narrator who withholds crucial information, speculates, questions, and withdraws periodically when the action is dramatized. This narrator refuses to make pronouncements, and in fact directly challenges readers to question, speculate, and decide for themselves. Why is the master-at-arms, John Claggart, moved to accuse the sailor of planning mutiny? Is he satanic, malicious, envious, suffering from self-hatred, perverted, mad? Why would the innocent sailor, Billy Budd, make himself guilty by striking his superior officer? Is he truly innocent or fatally flawed? Angelic or repressed? Heroic or naïve? And why would Captain Vere urge the court to discount Billy's intention and judge only the result of the deed? Is he narrowly bound to the rules of the navy? Caught in a tragic dilemma? Exercising tyrannical power? Unhinged? In an effort to tell the truth without compromising, Melville dramatizes the action and creates a narrator who challenges readers to think actively and attempt to judge honestly.

Scholarly interpretations of Melville's final short novel vary radically depending upon the interpreter's view of the central characters and the interpreter's sense of the form and tone of the novel. The work has been understood as a testament to Melville's acceptance of the ways of God and man, and a testament to his resistance, a tragedy and ironic social commentary, a political fiction and an essentially ambiguous text, among many others. Such themes as the conflict between civilization and the individual, capital punishment, and homophobia have also fascinated scholars as potential keys to the meaning of the novel. Deep and at times stylistically difficult, *Billy Budd, Sailor* is rich enough to support multiple readings and dense enough to deny any interpreter absolute certainty that he or she has arrived at the only truth about the book.

The essays selected for this literary companion provide teachers and students with a wide range of information and opinion about *Billy Budd* and about Melville's style, themes, and outlook on the human condition. The authors of the essays are noted professors at leading colleges and universities and/or scholars specializing in American literature and Melville studies. Each of the essays in this literary companion explains or discusses in detail a specific, narrowly focused topic, and the introduction to each essay previews the main points. The inserts that appear in selected essays exemplify ideas expressed by the authors or offer supplementary information. They are drawn from *Billy Budd, Sailor*, from critical commentary about the work, and from other literary sources.

The primary purpose of this companion is to enhance the reader's understanding and enjoyment of *Billy Budd, Sailor* as he or she strives to discern the elusive truth aptly embodied in this "ragged-edged" work of art. Perhaps Melville would have revised it more fully had he lived longer. Or perhaps he would have said, as Ishmael does in *Moby-Dick:* "God keep me from ever completing anything. This whole book is but a draught [draft]—nay, but the draught of a draught. Oh Time, Strength, Cash, and Patience!"[2]

NOTES

1. Herman Melville, *Billy Budd, Sailor (An Inside Narrative)*, ed. by Harrison Hayford and Merton M. Sealts Jr. Chicago: University of Chicago Press, 1962, p. 128.
2. Herman Melville, *Moby-Dick*, ed. Harrison Hayford and Hershel Parker. New York and London: W.W. Norton, 1967, p. 128.

FACTS AND FICTIONS: THE MAN WHO WROTE *BILLY BUDD*

Now recognized as one of America's preeminent nineteenth-century writers, Herman Melville lived the final years of his life in relative obscurity. Self-isolated from friends and virtually neglected by the literary establishment, but at last comfortably well-off, Melville retired from his position in the New York Custom House in late 1885. During his retirement, he gathered in his late poems memories of the friends and incidents of his early manhood. With a perspective earned through a long life marked by both success and suffering, Melville also drafted in his final years a last short novel. *Billy Budd* was dedicated to the friend of his youth, Jack Chase, and perhaps draws on incidents from his own life such as his fourteen months aboard an American man-of-war, his cousin's involvement in the *Somers* mutiny incident, and his father-in-law's controversial decisions on the Massachusetts bench. The tragically premature deaths of both of his sons may also have influenced Melville's final novel. Published posthumously, *Billy Budd* has been recognized by generations of readers and scholars as second only to the masterpiece of his early maturity, *Moby-Dick*.

EARLY LIFE AND EXPERIENCES AT SEA

The third of eight children, Herman Melville was born in 1819 into a distinguished family. His paternal grandfather, Major Thomas Melvill, had participated in the Boston Tea Party, and his maternal grandfather, General Peter Gansevoort, was a Revolutionary War hero. Herman's father, Allan, was a successful dry-goods merchant who unfortunately suffered a series of economic reversals during the depression of 1830. Allan Melville was forced to move his young family from New York City to Albany, where, heavily in debt to both Melville and Gansevoort relatives, he set himself up in the fur trade. By 1832 he was dead. Biographer James Barbour describes the conditions of Allan Melville's sudden demise: "In the dead of winter he traveled to New York on business: on his return he crossed the Hudson River on foot in below-zero temperatures. Tired, suffering from recent exposure, and harassed with financial concerns, he continued working. His health worsened. He soon lapsed into a state of excited delirium and died early in 1832."[1]

Herman was twelve when he lost his father and was forced to leave school to begin working. During the next seven years, he tried to contribute to the family income by working as a bank clerk, a farm laborer, a teacher, and a bookkeeper for his brother. He also studied surveying in hopes of procuring employment with the Erie Canal Engineering Department. He was not hired, however, so he instead went to sea. In 1839 Melville experienced life aboard the *St. Lawrence*, a merchant ship bound for Liverpool, England. After the disillusioning four-month trip, he followed his uncle, Thomas Melville, to Galena, Illinois, but returned to New York City in the fall of 1840. Unable to find work as a clerk, the twenty-one-year-old Melville signed on to serve as an ordinary seaman on the whaler *Acushnet*, which left New Bedford in January of 1841. The experiences of the next three years would furnish the material for Melville's first six books. In fact, Ishmael could be speaking for Melville when he says in *Moby-Dick* "a whale-ship was my Yale College and my Harvard."[2]

Although Melville had signed on for what he expected to be a three-year voyage, conditions aboard the *Acushnet* proved so brutal that Melville and his friend Toby Greene jumped ship in the Marquesas after eighteen months. Melville spent four weeks among the Typee, a tribe reputed to be cannibals, before the Australian whaler *Lucy Ann* appeared and Melville resumed his voyage as a whale man. Conditions aboard the *Lucy Ann* proved worse than those aboard the *Acushnet*, and Melville became embroiled in a mutiny attempt. He was jailed in Tahiti, but he and a friend, John B. Troy, were released when the *Lucy Ann* left port. They became "omoos," or rovers, spending several weeks roaming Tahiti and Eimeo. When he encountered the whaler *Charles and Henry*, Melville signed on as a harpooneer; he was discharged in Hawaii in 1843 and contracted himself as a clerk in Honolulu. When the *Acushnet*, the ship he had deserted the year before, arrived in Honolulu, Melville canceled his clerking contract and enlisted in the U.S. Navy on the frigate *United States.*

JOHN J. CHASE AND NEWS OF THE *SOMERS* MUTINY

Aboard the *United States,* Melville witnessed official floggings, which he considered part of the brutal legal code under which the navy operated. He also met John J. Chase. Biographer Tyrus Hillway describes Chase as "an Englishman with a bent for literature and adventure who delighted in quoting long passages from *The Lusiad.* John J. Chase had once deserted from the navy to fight on the side of Peru in its war against Bolivia. Pardoned because of his excellent record and known ability as a leader of men, he served as captain of the maintop"[3] when Melville met him. John J. Chase became one of Melville's heroes, the model for Jack Chase in the novel *White-Jacket,* and the man to whom Melville dedicated *Billy Budd.* Melville later described Chase as "a stickler for the rights of man and the liberties of the world."[4]

After serving less than a year aboard the *United States,* a notorious scandal occurred aboard the U.S. brig *Somers.* Perhaps Melville first heard the news of the scandal when his ship docked in Peru in December 1843. On the *Somers,* a training ship for apprentice officers, discipline was apparently more brutal than normal. Scholar Eric Homberger explains that in November 1842 the first lieutenant of the *Somers,* Guert Gansevoort (Melville's cousin), was informed that a mutiny was planned. The ringleader was alleged to be midshipman Philip Spencer, son of the U.S. secretary of war. "An informal court of inquiry was conducted by First Lieutenant Guert Gansevoort and the other officers, but they reported to the commander that the evidence did not appear conclusive."[5] Captain Alexander Mackenzie believed that the officers had misconstrued the evidence and, to protect the lives of all aboard ship, he urged the officers to reconsider their decision. Reluctantly, they convicted Philip Spencer, Elisha Small, and Samuel Cromwell of attempted mutiny. The three were hanged at the yardarm on December 1, 1842.

When Melville's ship docked in Boston in early October 1844, he certainly would have heard that the Naval Court of Inquiry had investigated the case and supported Mackenzie. He may also have read James Fenimore Cooper's furious denunciation of the scandal in his pamphlet "The Cruise of the

Somers: Illustrative of the Despotism of the Quarter-deck; and of the Unmanly Conduct of Captain Mackenzie." In making his accusations, "Cooper gave evidence to show why the First Lieutenant, Guert Gansevoort (Melville's cousin) deserved to be blamed for the injustice, along with the Captain,"[6] according to Lawrance Thompson. Guert gave his family a simple explanation: "I feel, that we did our duty; & the consciousness of having done my duty; shall ever sustain me. . . . Nothing was done 'in fear or haste'—& I believe it was approved of God; & I have faith to trust it will be by my fellow man."[7] Although Melville may have spoken with his cousin about the incident, no record remains of their conversation.

As a young man and a common sailor, Melville no doubt felt considerable sympathy for the common sailors so precipitously put to death on the *Somers.* As an older man, Melville reveals his sympathy for his cousin's position. In his poem "Bridegroom Dick," he mentions Guert by name and speaks also of a certain Tom Tight "no fine fellow finer," who "was lieutenant in the brig-o'-war famed/When an officer was hung for an arch-mutineer,/But a mystery cleaved, and the captain was blamed,/And a rumpus too raised, though his honor was clear." This same Tom Tight was no blabber even when drinking, but was "True to himself and loyal to his clan."[8] This divided sympathy perhaps elucidates the narrative tone in *Billy Budd,* sympathetic both to the young Billy, who is accused of planning mutiny and accidentally kills his superior officer, and to Captain Vere, who believes that Billy is essentially innocent yet urges his officers to execute the young man.

FIVE NOVELS AND A NEW FAMILY

At the age of twenty-five, Melville was back in New York and prepared to embark on a new series of adventures. Encouraged by his family to write down the stories of his life at sea, Melville wrote two best-sellers in three years. *Typee,* loosely based on his month among the Typee tribe, was published in 1846; *Omoo,* a fictionalized account of his wanderings in Tahiti, was published in 1847. For both books, Melville drew from his own experiences, but he also consulted numerous other sources of information to enhance his knowledge and his stories. This method of combining experience and research would become characteristic of Melville's later writing.

Successfully launched as a promising young author, Melville courted and married Elizabeth Shaw, daughter of Lemuel Shaw, chief justice of Massachusetts. The couple moved to New York City, where Melville met Evert Duyckinck, editor and founder of the journal *Literary World*. Melville was invited to Duyckinck's extensive library, and he became immersed in the adventure of self-education. As biographer James Barbour explains, "He avidly read Shakespeare as well as Dante, Montaigne, Coleridge, Browne, and Rabelais."[9] Melville's third novel, *Mardi*, published in 1849, reveals the results of his reading. The novel began as a story of his Pacific journeys but grew into a complex political allegory enlivened with metaphysical speculations on happiness, guilt, religion, and the ideal state. Although the book pleased Melville, it failed to appeal to readers, who were expecting another adventure story like the two earlier novels. *Mardi* did not sell well.

The Melvilles' first child, Malcolm, was born in the spring of 1849, and Melville was determined to support his family by writing. He composed two novels in the summer of 1849 specifically for the purpose of making money. Although Melville disdained both novels as mere "jobs," *Redburn* and *White-Jacket* are still read and appreciated today for foreshadowing the images and themes Melville would return to in such later works as "Bartleby, the Scrivener," "Benito Cerino," and *Billy Budd. Redburn* is loosely based on Melville's first short voyage to Liverpool and back aboard the merchant ship *St. Lawrence. White-Jacket*, a fictional reworking of Melville's experiences on the American man-of-war *United States*, has proven especially useful to interpreters of *Billy Budd*. In it, Melville created his ideal sailor, Jack Chase, modeled on John J. Chase, whom Melville had known aboard the *United States*. As the character White-Jacket says of Jack Chase, "The things which most men only read of, or dream about, he had seen and experienced."[10] Characteristically, Melville combined fact and fiction to create his characters and story. According to scholar John D. Seelye, Melville gives to Jack Chase not only attributes of John J. Chase but also experiences borrowed from the autobiography, "The Life and Adventures of John Nicol, Mariner" (1836). Resemblances between Jack Chase and Jack Gunn in William Leggett's tale "A Watch in the Main-Top" (1829) suggest to Seelye that Melville may also have read Leggett. Especially memorable in *White-Jacket* are the impassioned appeal against flogging and other naval abuses as well as the frightening list of offenses for which one could be put to death on a naval battleship. According to the articles of war listed in the novel, one could be put to death for thirteen different offenses, including making or attempting to make "any mutinous assembly"; disobeying the lawful orders of a superior officer, striking him, or drawing or raising any weapon against him; and "if any person in the Navy shall sleep upon his watch, he shall suffer death."[11] The articles of war figure prominently in *Billy Budd* as well.

While Melville was seeking publishers for these two "jobs" and relishing the opportunity to return to the sort of writing that he truly believed in even if it didn't pay well, his father-in-law, Judge Lemuel Shaw, was involved in two controversial court cases. According to Leonard Levy, Judge Shaw had "made his name a synonym for integrity, impartiality, and independence. Towering above class and party, doing everything for justice and nothing for fear or favor, he was a model for the American judicial character."[12] However, as Professor Brook Thomas suggests, Shaw, like Captain Vere in Melville's *Billy Budd*, "is a fair and honest man who unwittingly helps to maintain an unjust social order."[13] Judge Shaw, the foremost judge in Massachusetts, had gone out of his way to help runaway blacks achieve their freedom because of his personal abhorrence of slavery; however, after the passage of the 1850 Fugitive Slave Act, Shaw ruled in favor of returning runaway slave Thomas Sims to the South. Although Shaw's ruling seemed inconsistent with his earlier efforts to find any loopholes in the law that would provide a way to help runaway slaves, Professor Thomas points out that Shaw's decisions in each case were to uphold the letter of the law. The 1850 law closed loopholes in the 1793 Fugitive Slave Act, so Shaw felt bound to uphold the new law.

The homicide trial of Harvard Medical School professor John White Webster was equally controversial in 1850. Webster was accused of murdering and dismembering Dr. George Parkinson, who had recently financed the medical school. "When Webster was found guilty there was a general outcry, much of it directed against Shaw because of his charge to the jury. . . . According to common-law tradition, the commission of homicide had to be proved by direct evidence beyond the least doubt. Once the fact of homicide was established, the prosecution had to demonstrate beyond a reasonable doubt that the defendant committed the crime. In his charge to the jury, however, Shaw required only that the commission of homicide be proved beyond a reasonable doubt,"[14] writes Thomas. Shaw was accused of manufacturing law to suit the occasion, and even after Webster confessed, Shaw was condemned for veering from the path of judicial integrity. Supporters, on the other hand, pointed out that Shaw, who was socially acquainted with Webster, was quite sympathetic to Webster and had experienced great difficulty making his judgement. He is recorded as saying, "Nothing but a sense of imperative duty imposed on us by the law, whose officer and ministers we are, could sustain us in pronouncing such a judgment."[15] Perhaps, as Thomas suggests, Melville was remembering his father-in-law's dilemmas and decisions when he created his own Captain Vere forty years later.

MOBY-DICK

After the strain of writing quickly for money, Melville began his sixth novel, his mythic masterpiece *Moby-Dick*. Drawing from his experiences aboard three whaling ships, as well as his avid reading, this novel became an encyclopedic, epic masterpiece. *Moby-Dick*, written when Melville was in his early thirties, is an unprecedented achievement. Professor Carolyn L. Karcher describes Melville's whale of a novel:

> Conferring epic dignity on a class of men hitherto barred from the purview of literature, and elevating their despised occupation, the whale hunt, to mythic stature, *Moby-Dick*'s matchless achievement was to transform the implements, raw materials, and processes of a lucrative, gory industry, which subsisted on the plunder of nature, into rich symbols of the struggle to fulfill humanity's potential under conditions threatening apocalyptic destruction. The book's Shakespearean grandeur, philosophical depth, and daring mixture of genres and forms reflected Melville's omnivorous reading since entering literary circles.[16]

Melville dedicated the book to fellow writer Nathaniel Hawthorne, whom he had met in the Berkshires in the summer of 1850 and with whom he corresponded until late 1851. Melville had discovered in Hawthorne's work a quality that he also admired in Shakespeare's tragedies, "a great power of blackness,"[17] and he discovered in Hawthorne the man, a kindred spirit, someone with whom he could discuss ideas. In a letter to Hawthorne dated June 1851, Melville praises

Hawthorne's story "Ethan Brand" for its "frightful poetical creed that the cultivation of the brain eats out the heart," and even though he is exuberant in the letter about his own developing intellect, he states, "To the dogs with the head! I had rather be a fool with a heart, than Jupiter Olympus with his head."[18] The truths of the heart do not put supper on the table, however, and as Melville says in the same letter, "Try to get a living by the Truth—and go to the Soup Societies. Heavens! . . . Dollars damn me; and the malicious Devil is forever grinning in upon me, holding the door ajar. . . . What I feel most moved to write, that is banned, it will not pay. Yet, altogether, write the *other* way I cannot, so the product is a final hash, and all my books are botches."[19] Melville was clearly torn between his desire to reveal the truth through his fiction and his equally strong need to appeal to the reading public. The encouragement and friendship of Hawthorne, whom Melville admired as a genius, no doubt inspired Melville to complete the great whale book even if he wasn't fully satisfied with it. By the time *Moby-Dick* was published, in November 1851, the two writers had become mysteriously estranged. Predictably, *Moby-Dick* disappointed the admirers of *Redburn* and *White-Jacket.* Although the vast amount of information on whales and the whaling industry was praised by all early reviewers, the characterizations of Ahab, Ishmael, and the harpooneers were condemned as unrealistic, too like characters in German melodrama, or too full of ravings. The writer of such lunacy deserved a writ of *de lunatico,* an anonymous reviewer suggested.

MENTAL, PHYSICAL, AND FINANCIAL STRESS

The birth of his second son, Stanwix, on October 22, 1851, prompted Melville to begin work immediately on a seventh novel, which he apparently hoped would be popular. *Pierre: or the Ambiguities* was set in New York City and had all the elements of a psychological romance, a genre that was selling well at the time. However, the self-destructive impulses of the central character, the tendency of the novel to turn inward upon itself, and the reckless and bitter account in the novel of Melville's own literary fortunes, led readers to pronounce the book immoral and the author insane. Melville's family worried that *Pierre* mirrored Melville's latent self-destructive impulses, and his physical health was clearly deteriorating. Weakening eyes in addition to crippling sciatica and rheumatism soon forced Melville to seek a less stressful occupation.

By the time Elizabeth (Bessie) was born in 1853, Melville had begun a new career as a writer of short stories and serially published novels. Between 1853 and 1857, Melville became a successful magazine writer. He wrote stories for both *Putnam's Monthly Magazine* and *Harper's Monthly Magazine.* "Bartleby, the Scrivener" was the first and remains the most famous of Melville's stories. He also published serially *Israel Potter,* a historical novel which indicted America for its "failure to live up to its professed ideals";[20] "Benito Cerino," Melville's most powerful response to slavery and the blindness of both Northerners and Southerners; and *The Confidence-Man,* "a double-bitted satire, attacking gullibility in its first part and cynicism in its last."[21]

In 1855 Frances (Fanny), the fourth and last of the Melville children, was born. According to biographer Laurie Robertson-Lorant, Melville was a creative genius who at times suffered debilitating self-doubt and insecurity, which often resulted in his erupting in anger at his wife and children:

> Torn between the authoritarianism of his father's generation and the new generation's belief that loving guidance produced cheerful obedience, Melville was dangerously inconsistent with his children. When they were entertaining and did not challenge his authority, he could be affectionate and indulgent, but when they made demands or asserted their own wills, he could be emotionally withholding and tyrannical. Prone to baffling contradictions and dramatic mood swings . . . in our day he would almost certainly be diagnosed as manic-depressive. His use of alcohol as a muscle relaxant and painkiller probably increased his propensity to indulge, thus exacerbating the highs and lows to which he was subject, and deepening his depression.[22]

The stress Melville experienced while finishing *The Confidence-Man,* and the increasing distress his mood swings caused, led his wife to fear that Melville was nearing nervous collapse. Hoping to avert what threatened to be a breakdown, Melville's father-in-law, Judge Shaw, sent Melville abroad. In 1856–57, Melville traveled to England, Scotland, and the Holy Land.

Upon his return, Melville, with restored spirits and energy, attempted to support his family by lecturing. Between 1857 and 1860, he delivered lectures on "Statues in Rome," "The South Seas," and "Travel," but during the third season he was offered only three speaking engagements, so he was forced to look for some other means of livelihood. Melville was unable to secure a naval appointment when the Civil War began because of persistent back and eye trouble, and Judge Shaw's sudden death of a stroke in 1861 added to the Melvilles' distress. An inheritance from Judge Shaw provided financial relief, but it could hardly counterbalance the grief. During the war, Melville visited the Virginia battlefields in search of a Gansevoort cousin, and after the war he published a collection of poems titled *Battle-Pieces* (1866). Although it is now ranked with Walt Whitman's *Drum-Taps* as one of the best collections of Civil War poems, in 1866 *Battle-Pieces* was disdainfully reviewed and sales were disappointing. One positive result of writing what were construed as patriotic verses was that Melville made himself eligible for a government appointment after the war.

Between 1866 and 1886, Melville worked as an assistant inspector at the New York Custom House. Although he was now earning a regular salary, the period was framed by personal tragedies. In 1867, Melville's oldest son, Malcolm, committed suicide at the age of eighteen. Malcolm, who had just joined the National Guard, slept with a loaded pistol under his pillow. For reasons that have never been determined, he arrived home very late on the night before his death, slept late and missed work the following day. When his father returned home from work and pushed in the bedroom door, he discovered his son dead, "a pistol in his right hand and a bullet hole in his right temple."[23] Melville's response was first to idealize Malcolm, which inadvertently pushed Stanwix away, and then to "brood over the sins of omission and of commission that had led up to Malcolm's death, trying to imagine what he could have done differently."[24] In 1886, Melville's second son, Stanwix, died of tuberculosis at the age of thirty-five in San Francisco, far from friends and family. Stanwix, who had traveled the world and tried numerous jobs, seldom wrote home, but had worried his mother when he was younger with reports of a hospital stay and a persistent cough. When Lizzie heard that he was in the hospital again for pneumonia, she was unable to go to him. Bessie, their daughter, had developed such severe rheumatoid arthritis that she needed help even getting dressed and eating. Stanwix died with no family by his side, and Lizzie was devastated.

Between these two tragic deaths, Melville worked in the

Custom House and immersed himself in writing. During this time he composed a long philosophical poem, *Clarel,* based on his trip to the Holy Land. As Barbour says, "The poem is about a religious pilgrimage taken by Clarel and a group of companions, but it actually examines the possibilities of religious faith in a century shaken by scientific discoveries and the questions raised by German Higher Criticism. Clarel's doubts, like Melville's, were not resolved."[25]

FINANCIAL STABILITY AND FINAL WORKS

A modest inheritance from Elizabeth's family made it possible for Melville to retire from the Custom House in December 1885. He was sixty-six years old. During the last six years of his life, Melville wrote three collections of poems and a final short novel. *John Marr and Other Sailors* was privately published in 1888, and *Timoleon* was privately published in 1891. *Weeds and Wildings,* dedicated to Elizabeth, and *Billy Budd, Sailor,* were left in incompletely revised manuscript form at the time of Melville's death in 1891. As Robert Milder explains, the *John Marr* collection includes poems celebrating "a vision of free-spirited camaraderie amid nature's hardships" and poems documenting "shipwrecks and disasters, often amidst the pride of life and usually accomplished through some hidden treachery of reef, iceberg, or oozy, weed-choked floating wreck."[26] The *Timoleon* collection focuses on the "renunciations and rewards"[27] of those devoted to truth and the question of whether fame is the result of a providential plan or chance. Both published volumes of poems reveal preoccupations that are also seen in *Billy Budd.* For instance, the poem "Jack Roy" is a eulogy for Jack Chase, and Guert Gansevoort figures prominently in "Bridegroom Dick." Truth is centrally at issue in *Billy Budd* also.

A confluence of events no doubt worked together to inspire Melville's final novel. His nostalgic reminiscences about people and events from long ago, especially Jack Chase and Guert Gansevoort, are clear from the collections of poems written at the same time. In the summer of 1888, a renewal of interest in the *Somers* mutiny incident was sparked by Lieutenant H.D. Smith's article in *American Magazine* supporting Mackenzie's decision. Journalist Gail Hamilton responded in a series of three articles titled "The Murder of Philip Spencer," which appeared in June, July, and August of

1889 in *Cosmopolitan*. She clearly indicted Guert Gansevoort as well as Mackenzie and the naval bureaucracy that supported him. Literary critic Michael Paul Rogin claims that the articles may have prompted Melville to reimagine "the familially based conflicts which the *Somers* mutiny had first brought to Melville's fiction forty years before."[28] The controversy over the *Somers* incident may also have prompted Melville to recall the controversial decisions made by his father-in-law, Judge Shaw, during that pivotal year, 1850. And perhaps "the memory of Malcolm's death revived by Stanwix's in 1886"[29] moved Melville to thoughts of outliving both sons, and possibly feeling guilty or responsible for the unfortunate ends of both. Author Martin Leonard Pops notes, "There is much anguish here, and one remembers that Melville outlived both his sons, neither of whom married: Malcolm, the more docile one, who died a suicide in Melville's own house in 1867 at twenty [Pops is incorrect here, Malcolm is eighteen] (Billy's age) and Stanwix, the rover, the more difficult son, who died alone in a San Francisco hospital in 1886 at thirty-five (Claggart's age). To what extent did Melville believe himself responsible for the deaths of his children? To what extent did he believe their deaths the sacrifice life exacted for his 'completion?'"[30] No one will ever know for sure, but the father/son relationship is alluded to in *Billy Budd*, and the fascinating triangular relationships between Billy, Claggart, and Vere may have arisen from Melville's reflection about his relationship with his own two sons.

Before he brought *Weeds and Wildings* to press and while he was still revising *Billy Budd*, Melville died of a heart attack on September 28, 1891. He was seventy-two years old. After his death, Lizzie, who outlived him by fifteen years, carefully sorted through his papers, made notations, and penciled in questions. She placed the manuscripts in a box for safekeeping, and when she died in 1905, her granddaughters, Eleanor and Fanny, became the custodians of the papers.

THE TEXT OF *BILLY BUDD*

Melville's heavily revised manuscript was first transcribed by Raymond Weaver and published in 1924. According to later editors Harrison Hayford and Merton M. Sealts Jr., Weaver's purpose "was to prepare a text for the general reader, rather than any sort of literal transcription."[51] As a result, Weaver exhibited considerable editorial independence;

the text also reveals that he worked quickly. "Where he found an interlined revision not easily legible, he sometimes adopted the canceled earlier reading rather than strain after the author's latest wording, or if such an 'illegible' revision was an addition, he simply ignored it. Sometimes he discarded a revision Melville had made, and restored an earlier wording he himself preferred."[52] Unintentionally, Weaver made several structural errors that were reproduced in the 1948 edition prepared by F. Barron Freeman. Freeman attempted a definitive text, but like Weaver mistook Mrs. Melville's handwriting for Melville's own, so both editors accepted "three discarded leaves as the 'Preface,'"[53] included two superseded leaves headed "Lawyers, Experts, Clergy," and titled the novel *Billy Budd, Foretopman,* rather than the penciled revision of the title on the first page of the narrative, *Billy Budd, Sailor (An inside narrative).* Freeman, following Weaver, also used *Indomitable* as the name for Vere's ship even though Melville's latest revisions reveal that he had changed the name to *Bellipotent.*

In the late 1950s, Hayford and Sealts began an independent transcription and analysis of the text. The result of their careful study was the 1962 Reading Text and Genetic Text, which was published by the University of Chicago Press. The reading text includes Melville's last revisions; the genetic text allows scholars to understand Melville's process of composition. It is now clear that Melville was writing a prose headnote for the ballad "Billy in the Darbies" that grew into a narrative about a mature captain of the gun's crew who was about to be hanged for mutiny. In what Hayford and Sealts identify as the second phase of composition, Melville introduced John Claggart, Billy's antagonist; modified Billy's character to that of a young man who was impressed from a merchant ship into the navy and is innocent of the charge of mutiny; dramatized Claggart's campaign against Billy; developed the character of the Dansker; and elaborated on Claggart's inner nature. The manuscript grew to 150 leaves. In the final phase of composition, the story grew from 150 to 351 leaves. Melville delineated, then revised, Vere's character, and worked on the trial, Vere's speech to the court, and the execution. He also reworked Claggart's character, changed the name of the ship, and revised the surgeon's role. The effect was to make Vere's character much more ambiguous; the result has been increased critical attention to Vere's character and Melville's intention when revising it.

RESPONSES TO *BILLY BUDD*

In the 1920s and 1930s, "book lovers and academics in search of something called American Literature"[34] rediscovered and lionized Herman Melville. Weaver's biography of Melville, D.H. Lawrence's assessment of Melville's work, and the discovery and publication of *Billy Budd* in 1924 contributed to this interest. During this Melville revival, the final novel was read as a "testament of acceptance," humanist acceptance of tragic necessity or sometimes Christian acceptance of the ways of God. This way of understanding the novel has proponents to the present day. In the 1950s, critics like Joseph Schiffman, Phil Withim, and Lawrance Thompson saw the novel as "ironic in mode, social or antireligious in content, and rebellious in posture."[35] The ironist position also finds numerous supporters today.

By the mid-1960s, critical interest shifted to political readings of the novel and legal examinations of Captain Vere's decisions. "The most pronounced thematic tendency was an increased skepticism toward the character and motives of Captain Vere,"[36] according to author Robert Milder. Milton R. Stern's examination revealed Melville's political conservatism, and Brook Thomas's Marxist reading in the 1980s clarified the ways in which laws legitimate the institutions and interests of the ruling group. While many of the political interpretations reveal the writer's own ideological position, some elucidate the character of Vere and open ground for reflecting on the degree to which a man "is the victim of his own ambiguities and inconsistencies, and of history."[37] The essentially ambiguous nature of the text became increasingly interesting to readers in the late 1970s. Barbara Johnson, for instance, interprets the work as a parable of different, mutually exclusive ways of reading in which Billy, Claggart, and Vere find their counterparts in acceptance critics, ironic readers, and those who understand that the context created for reading predetermines the outcome of the analysis. Other critics, like H. Bruce Franklin, strongly disagree and find the text "fundamentally unambiguous."[38]

Beginning in the 1970s and of increasing interest today is an effort to interpret *Billy Budd* in light of the volumes of poetry that Melville was composing at the same time as the novel. Exploring this literary context reveals Melville's nostalgia for the age of philosopher kings and a romantic past, as well as his "interest in worldly reputation and the trials and rewards"[39] of dedication to finding truth. Increased attentiveness to the actual structure of the work has convinced literary critics that Melville was not trying to create what new critics call spatial unity—which presumes discoverable patterns for interpretation—but instead was working to create what Robert Milder calls "temporal unity," a "disposition to allow one subject or theme to evolve from another, so that the coherence of the work came to reside in the process of thought that guided its unfolding and was visible in the fault lines of the final product."[40] In other words, Melville was satisfied with the thematic disjunctions in the novel, and, according to Milder, interpreters may find it increasingly important to see in the work "overlapping perspectives of myth, religion, history, politics, and psychology"[41] rather than limiting their focus and risk distorting the text.

BILLY BUDD ENTERS POPULAR CULTURE

Readers' continuing fascination with *Billy Budd* is clear not only in the number of scholarly articles and books that it continues to inspire, but also in its appeal to a more popular audience. In 1949, *Uniform of Flesh*, the Broadway play based on *Billy Budd*, written by Louis O. Coxe and Robert H. Chapman, was first produced. It was revised and presented as *Billy Budd* in 1951 at the Biltmore Theatre in New York City and had a successful run. "In 1951, too, came the premier of Benjamin Britten's opera, *Billy Budd*, with libretto by E.M. Forster; it opened late in the year at Covent Garden," writes Sanford E. Marovitz. "Enormously successful, the opera quickly became a standard in the repertory not only of the Royal Opera but of New York's Metropolitan Opera as well."[42] The Broadway play received greater notoriety when it was broadcast on television in May 1959 as part of the Dupont Show of the Month series. Peter Ustinov's 1962 film, based on the play, reached the widest audience. The film script was written by Ustinov, Dewitt Bodeen, and Robert Rosen. According to M. Thomas Inge, "Ustinov's Vere is appropriately sensitive, but strictly devoted to his duties as an officer in time of war; Robert Ryan is perfectly sinister as Claggart in one of the most credibly evil roles during his career as a heavy; Melvyn Douglas is well-suited by age and temperament to the Dansker's role as a prophet and seer into the darker recesses of the human soul; and Terence Stamp in his first and perhaps most accomplished role of his career is the innocent, good-natured peacemaker Billy Budd."[45]

In 1983 the WGBHL Public Broadcasting station in Boston aired a two-part version of *Billy Budd* written by Marvin Mandell for *The Spider's Web* program. And in 1995, the film *The Curse of the* Somers: *Billy Budd's Ghost Ship,* directed by George Belcher and narrated by Peter Coyote, was produced. It dramatized George and Jack Belcher's recent exploration to find the shipwreck of the U.S. brig *Somers;* it also explains the 1842 mutiny and the sinking of the ship in 1846 off the coast of Veracruz, Mexico, during the Mexican War.

READING *BILLY BUDD*

Billy Budd is one of those books that invites discussion and enriches and refines one's understanding with each rereading. It also sparks controversy and reveals the reader's own acknowledged and unacknowledged beliefs and biases. Above all, *Billy Budd* challenges our capacity to discern truth. As Melville himself says, "In this world of lies, Truth is forced to fly like a scared white doe in the woodland; and only by cunning glimpses will she reveal herself, as in Shakespeare and other masters of the great Art of Telling the Truth,—even though it be covertly, and by snatches."[44]

NOTES

1. James Barbour, "Melville Biography: A Life and the Lives," in *A Companion to Melville Studies,* ed. John Bryant. New York: Greenwood Press, 1986, p. 4.

2. Herman Melville, *Moby-Dick,* ed. Harrison Hayford and Hershel Parker. New York and London: W.W. Norton, 1967, p. 101.

3. Tyrus Hillway, *Herman Melville.* New York: Twayne, 1963, p. 38.

4. Herman Melville, *White-Jacket, or the World in a Man-of-War.* New York: Grove Press, 1959, p. 29.

5. Eric Homberger, "Melville, Lt. Guert Gansevoort and Authority: An Essay in Biography," in *New Perspectives on Melville,* ed. Faith Pullin. Kent, OH: Kent State University Press, 1978, p. 265.

6. Lawrance Thompson, *Melville's Quarrel with God.* Princeton, NJ: Princeton University Press, 1952, p. 117.

7. Quoted in Homberger, "Melville, Lt. Guert Gansevoort and Authority," p. 268.

8. Herman Melville, "Bridegroom Dick," in *Collected Poems of Herman Melville*, ed. Howard P. Vincent. Chicago: Packard, 1947, pp. 174–75.

9. Barbour, "Melville Biography," p. 7.

10. Melville, *White-Jacket*, p. 301.

11. Melville, *White-Jacket*, p. 280.

12. Quoted in Brook Thomas, "The Legal Fictions of Herman Melville and Lemuel Shaw," *Critical Inquiry*, September 1984, p. 39.

13. Thomas, "Legal Fictions," p. 39.

14. Thomas, "Legal Fictions," p. 40.

15. Quoted in Thomas, "Legal Fictions," p. 41.

16. Carolyn L. Karcher, "Herman Melville: 1819–1891," in *The Heath Anthology of American Literature*, vol. 1. Lexington, MA: D.C. Heath, 1990, p. 2,402.

17. Melville, "Hawthorne and His Mosses," in *Moby-Dick*, p. 540.

18. Melville, "To Nathaniel Hawthorne," in *Moby-Dick*, p. 557.

19. Melville, "To Nathaniel Hawthorne," p. 557.

20. Laurie Robertson-Lorant, *Melville: A Biography*. New York: Clarkson Potter, 1996, p. 345.

21. "Herman Melville," in *American Writers: A Collection of Literary Biographies*, vol. 3, ed. Leonard Unger. New York: Scribners, 1974, p. 91.

22. Robertson-Lorant, *Melville*, pp. 370–71.

23. Robertson-Lorant, *Melville*, p. 514.

24. Robertson-Lorant, *Melville*, pp. 516–17.

25. Barbour, "Melville Biography," p. 12.

26. Robert Milder, "Melville's Late Poetry and *Billy Budd:* From Nostalgia to Transcendence," in *Critical Essays on Melville's* Billy Budd, Sailor, ed. Robert Milder. Boston: G.K. Hall, 1989, p. 213.

27. Milder, "Melville's Late Poetry," p. 215.

28. Michael Paul Rogin, "The *Somers* Mutiny and *Billy Budd*," in *Subversive Genealogy: The Politics and Art of Herman Melville*. New York: Alfred A. Knopf, 1983, p. 295.

29. Peter L. Hays and Richard Dilworth Rust, "'Something Healing': Fathers and Sons in *Billy Budd*," *Nineteenth-Century Fiction*, December 1979, p. 327.

30. Martin Leonard Pops, *The Melville Archetype*. Kent, OH: Kent State University Press, 1970, p. 253.

31. Harrison Hayford and Merton M. Sealts Jr., eds., introduction to *Billy Budd, Sailor (An Inside Narrative)*, by Herman Melville. Chicago: University of Chicago Press, 1962, p. 13.

32. Hayford and Sealts, introduction, p. 14.

33. Hayford and Sealts, introduction, pp. 18–19.
34. John Bryant, "Introduction: A Melville Renaissance," in *A Companion to Melville Studies*, p. xviii.
35. Milder, introduction to *Critical Essays on Melville's* Billy Budd, Sailor, p. 5.
36. Milder, introduction, p. 8.
37. Milder, introduction, p. 11.
38. H. Bruce Franklin, "From Empire to Empire: *Billy Budd, Sailor*," in *Herman Melville: Reassessments*, ed. A. Robert Lee. London and Totawa, NJ: Vision Press and Barnes & Noble Books, 1984, p. 201.
39. Milder, introduction, p. 15.
40. Milder, introduction, p. 16.
41. Milder, introduction, p. 18.
42. Sanford E. Marovitz, "Herman Melville: A Writer for the World," in *A Companion to Melville Studies*, p. 748.
43. M. Thomas Inge, "Melville in Popular Culture," in *A Companion to Melville Studies*, p. 709.
44. Melville, "Hawthorne and His Mosses," p. 542.

CHARACTERS AND PLOT

THE CENTRAL CHARACTERS

Billy Budd: The title character is twenty-one years old, innocent, illiterate, and a foundling. He stutters when upset but
is otherwise the epitome of the "handsome sailor." He is
good-looking, good-natured, and well liked. Billy is returning to England on the merchant ship *The Rights of Man*
when he is impressed by the British navy and becomes a
foretopman on the warship *Bellipotent.*

Captain Vere: The Honorable Edward Fairfax Vere is a
bachelor of forty from an aristocratic family. An accomplished
naval officer, he also loves books and is popularly known as
"Starry Vere." His name suggests verity or truth; in Latin, *vir*
means man; the homonym *veer* is also suggested by his name.
Vere is captain of the British warship *Bellipotent.*

John Claggart: The thirty-five-year-old master-at-arms
on the *Bellipotent* is an intellectual about whose past history
no one knows. Dark haired and pale, he is driven by a mysterious antipathy to Billy. Although he appears rational, his
monomania may be a result of innate depravity.

THE MINOR CHARACTERS

The Dansker: The old, wrinkled, experienced sailor originally from Denmark calls Billy "Baby" Budd and answers
his questions with cryptic pronouncements that Billy cannot
understand. The Dansker is compared to the Delphic oracle,
Merlin, and Chiron.

Squeak: Claggart uses this corporal to set petty traps for
Billy. Squeak also misreports Billy's behavior and words to
feed Claggart's antipathy. He is called Squeak because he resembles a rat ferreting about in the dark.

The Surgeon: He verifies that Claggart is dead, wonders
about the secrecy Vere insists on following the death, and
also wonders if Vere is unhinged.

The Purser: He considers Billy's death a phenomenon and wonders if it is willpower or euthanasia that allowed him to die so peacefully.

The Chaplain: He speaks with Billy the night before his execution, realizes that Billy's innocence is better preparation for death than mature Christian consolation, and kisses Billy on the cheek before leaving him.

The Drumhead Court: The council of officers that Vere appoints to try Billy is composed of the first lieutenant, the captain of the marines, who is called Mr. Mordant, and the sailing master.

Numerous Other Sailors: Captain Graveling is captain of the merchant ship *The Rights of Man,* and he mentions Red Whiskers who once punched Billy and is soon reconciled to him. Of the others on the *Bellipotent,* several are mentioned by name: Mr. Wilkes, the midshipman; Donald, a friend of Billy's who is later mentioned in the ballad; Albert, the hammock-boy or valet for Captain Vere; and Red Pepper, a red-haired, red-faced forecastleman.

THE PLOT

Billy Budd, Sailor, is set aboard the British warship *Bellipotent* in the summer of 1797, when England is at war with Revolutionary France. In the months just prior to the action of the novel, two mutinies have occurred aboard British ships: one at Spithead in the English Channel and another at the Nore near the mouth of the Thames River.

The central action of the novel can be outlined briefly. A young foretopman, Billy Budd, is impressed (drafted) into the British navy from a homeward-bound merchant ship. Soon after, he is falsely accused by the master-at-arms (naval chief of police), John Claggart, of fomenting mutiny. Inhibited by a stutter from answering the charge verbally, Billy strikes Claggart on the forehead once, killing him instantly. Captain Vere, the only witness, understands Billy's essential innocence and Claggart's malice, but he convenes a drumhead court (officers' council) and directs the court to judge the deed (striking and killing a superior officer), not the intention; Vere also urges the court to consider the consequences of acquittal (possible mutiny). The court reluctantly sentences Billy to death. Vere privately explains the verdict to Billy, and Billy is apparently reconciled to it since his final words are "God bless Captain Vere." Shortly after Billy's execution, the *Bellipotent* meets and captures the French vessel *Athee* (atheist). During the struggle, Vere is seriously wounded; he dies on shore saying "Billy Budd, Billy Budd."

The structure of Melville's short novel roughly approximates the five-part dramatic structure of a tragic drama: introduction, rising action, crisis, falling action, and catastrophe. The first eight chapters form the introduction to the central characters and situation. Billy Budd is presented as an example of the "handsome sailor" and as a peacemaker aboard the merchant ship whose captain reluctantly relinquishes him to the navy. After a digression on the mutinies at Spithead and the Nore and a digression on Admiral Nelson, Captain Vere is introduced. The portrait of the mysterious master-at-arms, John Claggart, closes the introductory sequence.

Chapters nine through seventeen present the rising action in which the central conflict between Billy and Claggart is developed. This section of the novel is focused on two incidents, Billy's accidental spilling of his soup and the troubling words of an afterguardsman to Billy late one night. The Dansker warns Billy that the master-at-arms is "down on" him and that the afterguardsman is a "cat's paw" for Claggart, but Billy is too innocent to understand. The narrator explores Claggart's character, attempting to probe his mysterious antipathy to Billy.

The crisis occurs in chapters eighteen and nineteen. In chapter eighteen, Claggart announces to Vere that he suspects Billy of planning a mutiny. In chapter nineteen, Vere attempts to test what he suspects is false witness by forcing Claggart to repeat his accusation directly to Billy. Billy strikes and kills Claggart.

Chapters twenty through twenty-two are focused on the deliberations of the drumhead court and the narrator's speculations about how Vere explains the verdict to Billy. This section can be called the falling action since it concentrates on the forces opposing Billy.

The next five chapters, twenty-three through twenty-seven, form the sequence surrounding the catastrophe, the hanging of Billy. The sequence is composed of two chapters focused on Billy's final night, one chapter on the hanging itself, and two chapters on the responses to Billy's death and burial, first from the surgeon and purser and then from of the crew.

Melville destabilizes the ending by adding three final chapters, which he calls a sequel. Chapter twenty-eight focuses on Vere's death. Chapter twenty-nine is the "official" report of the central incident, which villifies Billy and reveals Claggart to be the heroic victim. The last chapter includes both the sailors' deification of Billy and the ballad, "Billy in the Darbies."

CHAPTER 1

The Plot and Characters of *Billy Budd*

Melville's Manuscript Reveals How the Plot and Characters Evolved

Merton M. Sealts Jr.

In the last years of his life Herman Melville was writing and revising his final short novel, *Billy Budd, Sailor.* When he died in 1891, he left a disordered and heavily revised manuscript. Melville's grand-daughter shared the manuscript with a graduate student from Columbia University, Raymond Weaver, who made the first attempt to transcribe Melville's final work. When Weaver's edition was printed in 1924, *Billy Budd* was instantly recognized as a literary classic. Many editions and reprintings of the work followed. In the late 1950s professors Harrison Hayford and Merton M. Sealts Jr. began a new transcription and analysis of Melville's manuscript, which was published in 1962 and is now recognized as the standard transcription. It corrects the errors and oversights of the earlier editions and traces the evolution of the manuscript from a short prose introduction to the ballad "Billy in the Darbies" to the novel, *Billy Budd.*

In this selection from his 1983 lecture, "Innocence and Infamy: *Billy Budd, Sailor,*" University of Wisconsin professor and co-editor of the standard transcription Merton M. Sealts Jr. provides a synopsis of the plot and describes the three major phases of Melville's composition. Sealts explains that Melville concentrated first on creating Billy's character, then developed Billy's antagonist, John Claggart. Captain Vere was the product of Melville's last phase of composition. The manuscript reveals that Melville was retouching Claggart's character and revising Vere's when he died.

Excerpted from "Innocence and Infamy: *Billy Budd, Sailor,*" by Merton M. Sealts Jr., *A Companion to Melville Studies,* edited by John Bryant (New York: Greenwood Press, 1986). Copyright © 1986 by Greenwood Press. Reprinted with permission.

Billy Budd, Sailor, not only sums up the thought and art of Melville's last years but also looks back in setting, characterization, and theme over his writing as a whole. Left in manuscript at his death in 1891 and unpublished until 1924, *Billy Budd* has since appeared in many editions and printings, including over a score of translations. It has generated an extensive body of strikingly divergent commentary whose opposite poles are readings in terms of either personal tragedy or ironic social commentary.

The manuscript of *Billy Budd,* which Melville's widow described as "unfinished," comprises 351 leaves in her husband's crabbed hand, written partly in ink and partly in pencil, with some passages heavily revised; no printer could have worked directly from such disordered copy. The "Genetic Text" published by the University of Chicago Press in 1962 is now considered the standard transcription; other versions, especially those published in earlier years, differ significantly in their readings. Analysis of the manuscript has disclosed that Melville's story evolved in three major phases of composition, together with other less clearly defined stages and sub-stages. In general terms, the first phase involved concentration on Billy himself as protagonist, the second phase either introduced John Claggart or at least brought him to the fore as Billy's antagonist, and the third phase developed Edward Fairfax Vere as the sea commander under whom Billy is tried, convicted, and executed. This order of development, it might be noted, anticipates that of later critical discussion of the story, which also concentrated first on Billy, then on Claggart, and ultimately on Captain Vere.

SYNOPSIS OF THE PLOT

Melville's title character is a handsome sailor "aged twenty-one, a foretopman of the British fleet toward the close of the last decade of the eighteenth century," when Great Britain was at war with post-revolutionary France. We see him first aboard a homeward-bound English merchant ship, the *Rights-of-Man,* which is stopped by a British naval vessel seeking additional crewmen through forcible impressment. The warship bears another allegorical name: H.M.S. *Bellipotent,* or "warpower." The boarding officer selects Billy Budd, who is immediately transferred from the *Rights-of-Man* to the *Bellipotent* and inducted into the King's service. Already an accomplished seaman, Billy attracts favorable notice from both officers and sailors, with a single exception: John Claggart, master-at-arms, who serves aboard the ship as a nautical chief of police. Claggart's inherently evil nature is both drawn to and repelled by Billy's "good looks, cheery health, and frank enjoyment of young life." The two men stand in sharp contrast as types of innocence and worldly experience. Unlike Claggart, Billy in the "simplicity" of his youthful goodness has never willed malice nor been inflamed by the jealousy that possesses the master-at-arms as he looks enviously upon the Handsome Sailor.

After failing in an attempt to entrap Billy through an intermediary, who is sent to offer Billy money if he will turn mutineer, Claggart goes to the *Bellipotent*'s captain, falsely charges Billy with fomenting mutiny, and repeats the accusation to Billy himself during a confrontation in Captain Vere's cabin. Amazed and horrified by the groundless charge, Billy is unable to speak and defend himself as the captain urges him to do; a vocal impediment that afflicts him in time of stress produces only "a convulsed tongue-tie," and he lashes out with his fist, striking his accuser dead with a blow to Claggart's forehead. Vere, disbelieving Claggart's charge against Billy, is nevertheless aware that the young sailor, while innocent of mutiny, has in fact struck and killed a superior officer. In the captain's own words, Billy's deed is "the divine judgment on Ananias" delivered by "an angel of God"—yet that angel "must hang." Death by hanging is the sentence subsequently imposed upon Billy by the drumhead court that Vere quickly convenes, and the Handsome Sailor is hanged at dawn from a yard-arm of the mainmast before the entire ship's company. "At the penultimate moment, his words, his only ones, words wholly unobstructed in the utterance, were these: 'God bless Captain Vere!'"

Although the *Bellipotent*'s crew involuntarily echo Billy's blessing, their first response soon gives way to a threatening murmur that is promptly quelled by a strategic command from the quarter-deck. A similar murmur that arises following Billy's burial is also quieted by a drum-roll to quarters, "and toned by music and religious rites subserving the discipline and purposes of war, the men in their wonted orderly manner dispersed to the places allotted them when not at the guns." "With mankind," Vere would say, "forms, measured forms, are everything." Both Billy and Claggart are dead, and Vere's death is soon to follow. In an encounter between the *Bellipotent* and a French warship, the *Athée* (or *Atheist*—a third allegorical name), the captain receives a fatal wound and dies ashore at Gibraltar, "cut off too early" for a part in Horatio Nelson's memorable victories over the French at the Nile and Trafalgar. Not long before his death he is heard to murmur "words inexplicable to his attendant: 'Billy Budd, Billy Budd.'"

Among contrasting references to Billy and his fate that conclude the story, one, a journalistic account purportedly appearing in "a naval chronicle of the time," exactly reverses the truth, calling Billy the ringleader of a mutiny who, when arraigned before his captain by the master-at-arms, stabs his accuser to the heart and subsequently pays the penalty of death for his crimes. The other, a sailor's ballad entitled "Billy in the Darbies," expresses in rough but eloquent verse "the general estimate" among Billy's own shipmates of "his nature and its unconscious simplicity." These contradictory verdicts on the Handsome Sailor are summed up in a brief comment that Melville himself wrote in and then deleted from his manuscript. Such a story, he observed, is "not unwarranted by what sometimes happens" in the actual world—a world which, like the writer in the "naval chronicle," cannot distinguish between "Innocence and infamy, spiritual depravity and fair repute.". . .

"BILLY IN THE DARBIES" AND *BILLY BUDD, SAILOR*

The retrospective and even elegiac tone that marks Melville's last prose narrative also characterizes his third published volume of poetry, *John Marr and Other Sailors,* completed after his retirement from the customs service at the end of 1885 and privately printed in 1888. As we now know, Melville began *Billy Budd, Sailor,* in the course of his work on the *John Marr* volume, for which the ballad entitled "Billy in the Darbies" that now concludes the story was originally intended. . . .

Melville, as we now know, first thought of his speaker in the ballad not as young Billy but as an older man apparently guilty of fomenting mutiny, the crime for which he has been condemned to hang.

As with both "John Marr" and "Tom Deadlight [another poem in the *John Marr* volume]," Melville drafted a prose headnote to the ballad—and as with the earlier *Burgundy Club* pieces, the headnote grew in length until it far overshadowed the short verse it was intended to introduce. Removing the ballad from his projected volume, Melville then developed the burgeoning headnote into what became *Billy*

"BILLY IN THE DARBIES"

Billy Budd, Sailor *grew from a short prose headnote Melville wrote to introduce the ballad, "Billy in the Darbies." Both ballad and headnote were originally intended for the volume of poetry* John Marr and Other Sailors. *Melville placed a revised version of this ballad at the close of* Billy Budd, Sailor.

Good of the chaplain to enter Lone Bay
And down on his marrowbones here and pray
For the likes just o' me, Billy Budd.—But, look:
Through the port comes the moonshine astray!
It tips the guard's cutlass and silvers this nook;
But 'twill die in the dawning of Billy's last day.
A jewel-block they'll make of me tomorrow,
Pendant pearl from the yardarm-end
Like the eardrop I gave to Bristol Molly—
O, 'tis me, not the sentence they'll suspend.
Ay, ay, all is up; and I must up too,
Early in the morning, aloft from alow.
On an empty stomach now never it would do.
They'll give me a nibble—bit o' biscuit ere I go.
Sure, a messmate will reach me the last parting cup;
But, turning heads away from the hoist and the belay,
Heaven knows who will have the running of me up!
No pipe to those halyards.—But aren't it all sham?
A blur's in my eyes; it is dreaming that I am.
A hatchet to my hawser? All adrift to go?
The drum roll to grog, and Billy never know?
But Donald he has promised to stand by the plank;
So I'll shake a friendly hand ere I sink.
But—no! It is dead then I'll be, come to think.
I remember Taff the Welshman when he sank.
And his cheek it was like the budding pink.
But me they'll lash in hammock, drop me deep.
Fathoms down, fathoms down, how I'll dream fast asleep.
I feel it stealing now. Sentry, are you there?
Just ease these darbies [handcuffs] at the wrist,
And roll me over fair!
I am sleepy, and the oozy weeds about me twist.

Herman Melville, *Billy Budd, Sailor (An Inside Narrative)*, ed. by Harrison Hayford and Merton M. Sealts Jr. Chicago: University of Chicago Press, 1962.

Budd, Sailor, his final venture in prose fiction, with the ballad headed "Billy in the Darbies" standing as its conclusion. . . .

BILLY AND CLAGGART

As Melville's narrative of the condemned sailor developed apart from the *John Marr* volume, he altered his original conception of his title character as an older man, laying particular stress on a younger Billy's lack of worldly experience and delineating his appearance and character accordingly. In the story he is presented as "much of a child-man"; the old Dansker's nickname for his young friend is "Baby.". . .

In the expanded story young Billy appears as a fine physical specimen—a "Handsome Sailor"—but an inexperienced moral innocent, one who on either count might well have "posed for a statue of young Adam before the Fall." He is repeatedly likened both to other "young" figures of antiquity—Alexander, Achilles, David, Joseph, and Isaac—and to the sailor companions of Melville's own youth. The reminiscing John Marr regards all sailors as "Barbarians of man's simpler nature"; Billy too has a "simple nature," and the narrator twice calls him a "barbarian," implicitly associating him not only with sailors but also with those uncivilized and un-Christianized Polynesians described in *Typee* and *Omoo* [earlier novels by Melville], victims of what passes for Christian civilization. Melville, it has been aptly said, [by F.O. Matthiessen] "had thought of unspoiled barbarians at every stage of his writing since *Typee,*" and in *Billy Budd* he specifically compares Billy's attitude toward the Chaplain's religion to that of a "superior *savage,* so called—a Tahitian, say, of Captain Cook's time or shortly after that time." In both his appearance and his character Billy with his "simple nature" is thus reminiscent of all youthful, unenlightened, and even "savage" characters in Melville's writings from *Typee* onward.

When Melville turned from Billy to Claggart, the second of his major characters to emerge as the story developed, he in a sense moved from the world of *Typee* and *Omoo* to that of *Redburn* and *White-Jacket,* for Claggart is a further development of such figures in the latter books as Jackson and Bland. Thematically, he is the antithesis of Billy, for he is a man "dominated by intellectuality" who finds civilization "auspicious"; the two of them are paired as Jackson is paired with young Redburn, or Radney in *Moby-Dick* with Steelkilt, and to think of the one figure apparently led Melville to conceive of its opposite as well.

Claggart and his "mystery of iniquity" presented more difficulty in characterization than did the simpler Billy. "His portrait I essay," the narrator remarks of Claggart, "but shall never hit it," and as the manuscript reveals, Melville was still in the process of retouching that portrait when he put work aside during his last illness. In seeking to get at Claggart's hidden nature he made explicit reference to both the Bible and Plato, and in writing of the man's mixture of envy and antipathy with respect to Billy he drew as well on such literary analogues as Shakespeare's Iago and Milton's Satan. Within the compass of Melville's own works, Claggart climaxes that long line of monomaniacs—men obsessed with one passionately held idea—that runs from Ahab in *Moby-Dick* through the subordinate characters in *Clarel,* to all of whom Melville had extended his sympathetic understanding, if not his approval.

CAPTAIN VERE

As in *Moby-Dick* he had ascribed "high qualities" and "tragic graces" to "meanest mariners, and renegades and castaways," so in *Billy Budd,* with Billy and Claggart, Melville initially created a drama played "down among the groundlings," its stage "a scrubbed gun deck." Insofar as *Billy Budd* is the story of these two antagonists, it has the democratic implications of Melville's earliest books, but with the emergence of Captain the Honorable Edward Fairfax Vere, the third and latest to develop of the story's three principal characters, the dramatic focus of its central chapters shifts from the gundeck to the captain's cabin.

Unlike Billy and Claggart, deriving as they do from antecedents in Melville's early books, Vere is the creation of an older writer—and a more conservative thinker, in the view of critics such as Milton R. Stern, Thomas J. Scorza, and Michael Paul Rogin; his affiliations are chiefly with the work of Melville's later years. The sea-captains of the earlier fiction, Ahab included, are typically autocrats; the occasional exceptions, like Amasa Delano and Benito Cereno, are special cases. During the Civil War, when Melville visited the battle-front and came to know senior military men, he seems to have formed a higher opinion of the officer class; his sketches of the 1870s concerning Major Jack Gentian and his depiction of Captain Turret in "Bridegroom Dick"—much less the martinet than Vere—are indications that he had indeed done so. But Captain Vere, it must be remembered, was created to fulfill the demands of Melville's plot, which required a senior officer to preside over young Billy's condemnation and carry out the sentence that he suffer death by hanging; Melville must therefore have asked himself the obvious question: What kind of man *could* and *would* do what Vere *must* do?

In his efforts to answer this question Melville was led into even more troublesome psychological probing than his analysis of Claggart entailed. Late revisions in those manuscript passages that deal with Vere's state of mind at the time of Billy's fatal blow testify that he was still retouching Vere's portrait as well as Claggart's when his last illness prevented further work on the story. As the manuscript stands, Vere appears, for good or for ill, as a supremely dedicated servant of King and country, first and foremost an officer enrolled in "the host of the God of War—Mars.". . .

As a defender of the old order against modern innovation, Vere again has much in common with Melville himself as seen in the writings of his later years: a man disenchanted with the prevailing faith in humanity's so-called progress— "Adam's alleged advance," as he had called it in the *Burgundy Club* sketches—who believed instead that human nature is essentially the same from age to age, regardless of superficial changes such as modern inventions and other supposed improvements. Both Vere and the reclusive Melville of the last decades of his life take more satisfaction in reading than in "social converse"; Vere loves "history, biography, and unconventional writers like Montaigne" as did Melville himself, and he too is "as apt to cite some historic character or incident of antiquity as he would be to cite from the moderns."

Another possible analogy between Vere and Melville turns on the captain's relation to Billy Budd. Given his favorable impression of the young sailor, he clearly disbelieves Claggart's charge that Billy has been fomenting mutiny, but he nevertheless arranges a confrontation between them. In a "fatherly" tone he encourages the vocally hesitant Billy to reply to Claggart, thus helping to precipitate the fatal blow by which Billy strikes Claggart dead. From then on, however, "the father" in Vere is "replaced by the military disciplinarian," but after the trial it is Vere himself, "old enough to have been Billy's father," who tells the young sailor of the verdict. . . .

[T]he ultimate subject of *Billy Budd*, it may well be, is death. But how to read that final story, as its narrator pointedly declares, "every one must determine for himself," and it is tempting to say that as many interpretations have been advanced as there have been readers and critics.

The Plot and Characters Are Allegorical

David Kirby

In this selection from his book *Herman Melville*, Professor David Kirby explains that the description of the characters, the names of the ships, and the biblical references throughout the work suggest that Melville was writing allegorically, on two levels at once. In other words, *Billy Budd* is not only a story about one incident at sea in 1797; it is also a suggestive retelling of the fall of man in the Garden of Eden in which Billy, Claggart, and Captain Vere have their counterparts in Adam, the Serpent, and God. Other biblical references intimate that Claggart is also like Ananias, the biblical liar who drops dead after lying to God; that Vere behaves like Abraham when commanded to sacrifice his son Isaac; and that Billy is like Christ when at his death he ascends into the morning sun illuminating clouds which are described as "the fleece of the Lamb of God." Kirby explains that it is also possible to read the work as psychological allegory in which the three central characters represent the ego, id, and superego battling within a single person; the novel could even be read as secular allegory in which the innocent orphan (Billy) is doomed by malign fate (Claggart) and helpless benevolence (Vere), Kirby suggests.

In addition to his book on Melville and several articles on Melville's short story, "Bartleby, the Scrivener," Kirby has written book-length studies of reconstruction writer Grace King, contemporary poet Mark Strand, and Henry James's works, *The Portrait of a Lady* and *The Turn of the Screw*. Kirby is a professor at Florida State University.

"Billy Budd" begins with a tribute to the concept of the Handsome Sailor, a fellow of strength and beauty tempered

Excerpted from *Herman Melville*, by David Kirby (New York: Continuum, 1993). Copyright © 1993 by David Kirby. Reprinted with permission.

by an equally well-developed moral nature and thus the idol of his shipmates. Such a one is Billy Budd, described in his initial appearance as "welkin-eyed," that is, blue-eyed, from a chiefly literary term meaning "sky" or, more properly, "vault of heaven." Also known as Baby Budd, Billy is a fore-topman serving in the British Navy at "the close of the last decade of the eighteenth century"; later, the date of the events in the story is given as 1797. Just before the narrative begins, Billy was impressed into service from an English merchantman bound for home to the ominously named HMS *Bellipotent* (warpowerful). A civilian, an infant, even, Baby Budd accepts his fate uncomplainingly, stepping care-lessly from one sort of life at sea to its complete opposite.

The merchantman's shipmaster complains of the loss; such a Handsome Sailor as Billy has not only been, by exam-ple, a peacemaker among his cantankerous crew but has even turned the men into a "happy family." In his innocence, Billy not only calls farewell to his friends but breaches naval deco-rum when he cries out to the merchantman itself, it, too, bear-ing a significant name. "And good-bye to you too, old *Rights-of-Man,*" cries Billy, and is instantly admonished by the naval lieutenant, who assumes the rigor of his rank, "though with difficulty repressing a smile." Though he has presumably surrendered the rights of man (Thomas Paine's book by that title is cited as the source of the merchantman's name), Billy is instantly taken up by the crew of the *Bellipotent* and soon begins to exert his benevolent influence there as well.

BILLY IS AN ALLEGORICAL CHARACTER

Billy does seem a bit too good to be true, and some readers have referred to his semidivine nature, particularly his mys-terious, godlike appearance on this earth. After all, Billy was not born but found, as he says, "in a pretty silk-lined basket hanging one morning from the knocker of a good man's door in Bristol." However, to say, on this basis, that his origin is miraculous is to overlook the presence of the other orphans in Melville, those figures who seem both blessed and cursed by their solitary states. To Melville, orphanhood functions as a reminder of the essential loneliness of all humanity, but it is also a necessary condition for the picaresque characters who give most of his fiction its drive. Being alone is not a happy state in Melville, but it is indispensable; "thought-divers" do not dive in pairs.

In one sense, though, Billy is radically different from the other orphans who populate Melville's pages. Whereas Tommo, Typee, and the others are cunning, shrewd, even mildly criminal in nature, Billy is utterly guileless. He is a perfect, or a near-perfect, creature, yet he is no god. Perhaps Billy is best described as the embodiment of the highest natural qualities; not quite a complete human being, Billy seems more like an allegorical representation of calm, good cheer, physical good looks, and an even, accepting temperament. The other two main characters are representations of other human qualities; together with Billy, as will be argued below, they more or less comprise a single fully-developed person.

So while it would be wrong to view Billy as a literal demigod, it is clear that Melville is writing allegorically, connecting his character to a venerable religious and literary tradition in order to show that his story is an ageless drama rather than an isolated incident at sea. In typically teasing fashion, Melville notes that Billy is "not presented as a conventional hero, but also that the story in which he is the main figure is no romance." As he emphasizes what "Billy Budd" is not, he clearly invites us to say what it is. And among the most obvious possibilities is allegory.

Thus, in describing Billy's single physical flaw, Melville does so in a manner contrived to make the reader think of Genesis (and of his American master [Nathaniel] Hawthorne as well):

> Though our Handsome Sailor had as much of masculine beauty as one can expect anywhere to see; nevertheless, like the beautiful woman in one of Hawthorne's minor tales ["The Birthmark"], there was just one thing amiss in him. No visible blemish indeed, as with the lady; no, but an occasional liability to a vocal defect. Though in an hour of elemental uproar or peril he was everything that a sailor should be, yet under sudden provocation of strong heart-feeling his voice, otherwise singularly musical, as if expressive of the harmony within, was apt to develop an organic hesitancy, in fact more or less a stutter or even worse. In this particular Billy was a striking instance that the arch interferer, the envious marplot of Eden, still has more or less to do with every human consignment to this planet of Earth. In every case, one way or another he is sure to slip in his little card, as much to remind us—I too have a hand here.

REFERENCES TO THE GARDEN OF EDEN

It is shortly after this Eden reference that Melville introduces into the narrative the other main characters, both of whom recall their counterparts in Genesis. Captain the Honorable Edward Fairfax Vere presides over the *Bellipotent,* godlike and distant. He is identified as a scholar, a lover of antiquity, and, like the Master of Chancery [in Melville's story, "Bartleby, the Scrivener"] and Amasa Delano [in Melville's work, *Benito Cereno*], a bachelor. If he is the ship's brain, its muscle is John Claggart, the master-at-arms and thus "a sort of chief of police charged among other matters with the duty of preserving order." He is black-haired and pale-skinned; unlike the ordinary seamen, he spends most of his time in the shadows. Like Billy, Claggart too has a mysterious past; it is thought by some that he may not even be an Englishman. When he falsely accuses Billy of conspiracy, his eyes undergo "a phenomenal change, their wonted rich violet color blurring into a muddy purple. Those lights of human intelligence, losing human expression, were gelidly protruding like the alien eyes of certain uncatalogued creatures of the deep. The first mesmeristic glance was one of serpent fascination; the last was as the paralyzing lurch of the torpedo fish." If "welkin-eyed" Billy is associated with the heavens, Claggart is linked with the wet hell of the deepest seas, a realm of finny monsters.

The clash between Claggart and Billy comes as a complete surprise to the latter, whose innocent nature is devoid of the irony and cynicism that come so naturally to the other sailors. Melville observes that Claggart is the embodiment of "Natural Depravity," a condition of insanity that masks itself in the appearance of reason. Unlike other criminal types, the naturally depraved are born that way; they tend to be prideful, ascetic, and intelligent. Indeed, part of Claggart's malign motivation is that he is intelligent enough both to comprehend Billy's goodness and to know that he can never partake of it. It is this biting jealousy that leads Claggart to falsely accuse Billy of conspiracy to mutiny.

ADDITIONAL BIBLICAL REFERENCES

Claggart's charge and the events that follow take momentum from the anxious context in which they occur, for already that year there had been two notable mutinies in the British navy. Additionally, there are dissatisfied sailors aboard the *Bellipotent* whose cryptic mutterings only confuse Billy; it is suggested that at least one of them is a "cat's-paw" sent by Claggart to entrap the Handsome Sailor. This

troubled atmosphere gives weight to Claggart's false accusation of Billy, a charge the fair-minded Vere is inclined to
disbelieve. Vere does things by the book, however, and
rather than dismiss Claggart out of hand, he has him repeat
the charge in front of Billy, who, tongue-tied, strikes his accuser dead. Vere equates Claggart with Ananias, the biblical
liar, and says that he has been "'struck dead by an angel of
God! Yet the angel must hang!'" Even before he calls the
drumhead court, Vere knows what sentence is mandated by
naval regulations.

There are, of course, options: some of the officers urge
Vere to refer the matter to the fleet's admiral, and one of
them tries to establish Claggart's motive as a possibly miti-
gating factor. But as captain, Vere feels compelled to make
the decision himself and in accordance with maritime law
and specifically with the Articles of War that make striking
a superior officer a capital crime. He tells the other members of the drumhead court that he must "strive against
scruples that may tend to enervate decision. Not, gentlemen,
that I hide from myself that the case is an exceptional one.
Speculatively regarded, it well might be referred to a jury of
casuists. But for us here, acting not as casuists or moralists,
it is a case practical, and under martial law practically to be
dealt with." He also argues that the officers' allegiance is to
the King, not Nature, and tells them that their cool heads
must prevail over their warm hearts. When the others argue
that they might convict Billy yet mitigate the penalty, Vere
argues that they cannot.

Here is the crux of the story, the turning point at which
the narrative can continue to proceed inexorably toward
Billy's death or reverse itself and let the hapless sailor live.
Vere's argument is that the crew of the *Bellipotent* will think
mercy a sign of weakness and perhaps make the false
mutiny of which Billy was accused a reality. "Your clement
sentence they would account pusillanimous," he tells the
other members of the court. "They would think that we
flinch, that we are afraid of them. . . . I feel as you do for this
unfortunate boy. But did he know our hearts, I take him to
be of that generous nature that he would feel even for us on
whom . . . so heavy a compulsion is laid." Like the biblical
Abraham, Vere puts duty before feeling. And Billy's fate is
sealed.

Billy's last hours and execution are saturated with religious imagery, Christian and otherwise. The *Bellipotent*'s chaplain, "the minister of Christ though receiving his stipend from Mars," finds Billy in a peaceful, oblivious state, like a "superior *savage,* so called—a Tahitian, say, of Captain Cook's time." Convinced that Billy is utterly ignorant of religion yet as sure of Heaven as any of the faithful, the chaplain kisses him on his cheek and withdraws. Just before the hanging, Billy calls out, "God bless Captain Vere"; in the Handsome Sailor's last mortal act, he affects the crew so movingly that they repeat his words. The rope is tightened, and "at that moment it chanced that the vapory fleece hanging low in the East was shot through with a soft glory as of the fleece of the Lamb of God seen in mystical vision, and simultaneously therewith, watched by the wedged mass of upturned faces, Billy ascended; and, ascending, took the full rose of the dawn." Interestingly, as the soul of Billy merges with the morning sun as well as the Son of God, Vere is described as standing "erectly rigid as a musket in the ship-armorer's rack." Further miraculous events, or at least "phenomenal" ones (to use the term chosen by the surgeon and purser, who discuss the execution), ensue: Billy's body does not jerk in the death spasm but hangs motionless from the yard end. And upon his burial, seafowl fly screaming to the spot where his body disappears beneath the waves; this stands in marked contrast to the disposal of Claggart's remains, which sink unceremoniously.

OTHER ALLEGORICAL POSSIBILITIES

In this way Melville the literary confidence man seems to be teasing the reader again, here implying that Billy is in fact godlike. Indeed, that might be the reader's logical assumption were the story to end here, as it very well might. But Melville returns the focus to Captain Vere, who is wounded in a sea battle and dies with Billy's name on his lips. By returning to the Abraham-like Vere, Melville reminds us of the allegorical nature of the story. One might say that Billy, Claggart, and Vere are rough pre-Freudian equivalents of the ego, id, and superego. But it would be more appropriate to Melville's own day and to his particular worldview to see Billy as the orphan doomed through no real fault of his own, Claggart as the malign fate who crosses everyone's path sooner or later, and Vere as the benevolent, helpless figure who tries to live rightly and somehow manages to survive despite his good intentions. These elements mark most of Melville's fiction in one way or another. It is simply that, in "Billy Budd," Melville chose to draw on his considerable knowledge of lore to deck his story in the imagery of the oldest story of all, the one that is in the scripture of every culture—the story of the struggle between good and evil.

Snake Imagery Complicates Interpretations of Claggart

Jonathan Yoder

Although Claggart is commonly read as the personification of evil in *Billy Budd*, neither the character nor the concept of evil is simple, according to Northern Virginia Community College professor Jonathan Yoder. Claggart is specifically identified with the satanic snake in Eden who seduced mankind to disobey God, but Yoder explains that for Melville this Original Sin is not uniformly disastrous because mankind acquires knowledge as well as guilt. In fact, Melville was especially interested in a second-century Gnostic sect of Christians who venerated the snake as the source of wisdom in Eden. According to this heretical sect, Sophia (Wisdom) created the universe, became indignant when her son Yahweh claimed to be supreme, transformed herself into the serpent in Eden, and later became the Christ who provided knowledge about salvation and eternal life. The snake as a symbol of eternal life is prevalent in many Eastern religions as well as in Hebrew thought, Yoder explains. Moses, for instance, used the snake as a symbol of deity and healing while an alternate Hebrew image of deity was the fertility god Baal, portrayed as a bull. Interestingly, Claggart is associated with the snake and Billy is associated with the bull. While Claggart is snakelike, Yoder urges readers to resist simply dismissing him as the personification of evil.

Throughout decades of deliberations, the jury of readers has returned a consistently uniform verdict against the obvious

villain in Herman Melville's *Billy Budd.* John Claggart has
been found guilty as a one-dimensional personification of
evil who is specifically described as a serpent—the form Satan took to trick women (and thus men) into our original sin,
an act transformed in our collective memory into an ostensibly innate fear of snakes. . . .

The "issues" in the novel, according to John Seelye, "seem
somewhat simplified, and, though the opposition of Christly
Billy and Satanic Claggart is surely diagrammatic, it appears
almost melodramatic in its reduction of values." Similarly,
Michael Paul Rogin summarizes easily: "Claggart, a figure
of natural depravity to match Billy's natural innocence, is an
allegorical type as well." In his useful study of Melville's re-
liance on typology, John H. Timmerman concludes that
through the image of the snake Melville makes it "abun-
dantly clear" that "Claggart represents diabolical evil." For
David S. Reynolds, "Just as Billy is flawed but totally virtu-
ous, so Claggart seems civil but is totally evil. . . . [Billy's]
crime is justified because it is directed not against society
but against a satanic individual."

In this context most critics of *Billy Budd* reflect an orthodox version of Satan's role in human history, whether or not
they believe in the existence of a literal personification of
evil. For these critics the conflict is simple: Claggart is a
snake; the snake represents Satan; Satan represents evil.
Billy represents humanity in a state of innocence. Satan attacks and (depending on one's interpretation of Billy's "cru-
cifixion") successfully destroys Billy or destroys himself.

The simplicity of this perspective, however, distorts the
complexity of religious attempts to deal with sins and sin-
ners. From an alternative perspective *Billy Budd* can be
viewed as illustrating Melville's continual fascination with
the connection between human knowledge and human
guilt—a complex philosophical concept brilliantly symbolized in his last novel by his image of the snake. Far from
merely serving as a symbol for the presence and power of
darkness, "as the serpent represents any primeval, cosmic
force, it shares the ambiguity of all ancient, elementary symbols" [according to the *Dictionary of Symbols and Imagery*].
Thus, [as J. Schouten suggests] "the serpent has always
stood for two diametrically opposed ideas, namely as the foe
of mankind and the symbol of evil on the one hand, and as
man's protector and savior in disease and distress on the

other." Identification with a serpent, in short, need not lead to uncomplicated rejection of Satan or Claggart, although Satan and his logo, the snake, have received such concentrated doses of bad publicity that efforts to complicate the image run the risk of being identified as heretical. . . .

THE SNAKE AS A SYMBOL OF WISDOM

The snake, a symbol for wisdom in virtually every culture, played a role in the story of the Garden of Eden that fascinated Melville because the Fall can be described as movement from purity to sinfulness or from ignorance to knowledge. From the latter perspective, officially heretical, the Fall was fortunate.

This perspective did not begin with Melville, of course. From the Greek portrayal of Prometheus to contemporary deconstructors of literary texts who deny the unique validity of any single interpretation, there exists a tradition inside and outside orthodox Christianity that champions free inquiry (described by opponents as anarchy) over authoritative definitions of right and wrong. For Melville, the second-century Gnostics were influential contributors to that tradition. . . .

Thomas Vargish has clarified Melville's interest in the Gnostics, particularly the Ophite sect, defenders of the serpent as the source of *good* advice in the Garden of Eden. For the Ophites, to venerate the serpent was merely to pay homage to the "medium of divine revelation.". . .

Within this tradition Sophia (Wisdom) creates the universe; her son, who becomes Yahweh, is given control of the earth. As the creator God of the Old Testament, He claims to be supreme. Indignant, Sophia becomes a serpent to combat this audacity in Eden. As described by Joseph Campbell, Yahweh strikes back, giving Moses a set of laws that people could not possibly follow. The Serpent responds, returning to earth again as Christ (residing in Jesus) and providing knowledge of the possibility of salvation. . . .

Pierre contributes to an understanding of *Billy Budd*, as Charles Moorman has shown, by providing "the whole of Melville's philosophy" through "a consistent pattern of imagery existing on a level below the narrative." Pierre, early in the novel, is an innocent person living in his own Garden of Eden. Isabel takes on the role of the serpent . . . but "her influence is not wholly malign," according to Moorman, since "she is like the serpent as it appears as a messenger in more complex versions of the Fall." Thus Melville has prepared us for the snake in *Billy Budd*, which figures as a simultaneous destroyer of innocence and ignorance.

The alternative to innocent ignorance is guilt associated with knowledge. Claggart is one of those instances of depravity which have "no vulgar alloy of the brute in them, but invariably are dominated by intellectuality.". . .

Claggart had adequate knowledge of the world, or at least "his general aspect and manner were . . . suggestive of an education," and the narrator suspects that, "one person excepted [presumably Vere], the master-at-arms was perhaps the only man in the ship intellectually capable of adequately appreciating the moral phenomenon presented in Billy Budd." If Claggart can appreciate Billy as a moral phenomenon, an abstract concept, why does he find it impossible to appreciate Billy as a human being, developing the positive sort of relationship that evolved so naturally between Billy and the rest of the crew? Melville's answer to that question, key to his characterization of Claggart, is ambiguous. To understand a character for whom "the method and the outward proceeding are always perfectly rational," Melville suggests, one is obliged to contemplate human nature as a mysterious mixture of good and evil. Knowledge may seem desirable, but acquisition of knowledge does not make man good. Something else is inherent in human nature, something described in "Holy Writ in its phrase 'mystery of iniquity,'" a concept missed by those who find in Claggart allegorical simplicity. Thus the mysterious aspect of original sin—acquisition of knowledge—inheres in the human suspicion that this central crime is also the key to any positive conclusions we might reach about human nature. . . .

THE SNAKE AS A SYMBOL OF LIFE

The history of the snake as a symbol of life is as long, though not as dominant, as its history as a symbol for death. According to Barbara G. Walker, the Hindus, Chinese, Greeks, and Melanesians all initially saw the snake as a symbol of eternal life. "A basic serpent-myth said the dual Moon-goddess of life and death made the first man. Her bright aspect suggested making him immortal like the snake, able to shed his skin; but her dark aspect insisted that he should die and be buried in the earth." Walker also notes that the "early Hebrews adopted the serpent-god all their contemporaries revered, and the Jewish priestly clan of Levites were 'Sons of the Great Serpent,' i.e. of Leviathan 'the wiggly one.'" Balaji Mundkur adds: "Mythic monsters like Leviathan, the sea serpent Rahab, the 'coiled serpent' and the 'fiery serpent' are just as much a part of Israelite religious heritage as the despised temples of Eden and symbol of Satan."

While it is not necessary to point out Melville's use of Leviathan or Rahab, critics (though aware of his thorough familiarity with the Bible) have failed to notice the Old Testament conflict between those for whom God was to be venerated as the Great Serpent, Nehustan, and those who preferred the image of the fertility god of Canaan, Baal, routinely portrayed as a calf or bull.

THE SNAKE AND THE BULL

As the religion of the Children of Israel developed into monotheism, it went through stages in which it merely claimed to have a God that was superior to all regional alternatives. To prove access to divine power, for example, Aaron turned his rod into a snake before Pharaoh's eyes. Pharaoh's magicians matched this feat: "For they cast down every man his rod, and they became serpents: but Aaron's rod swallowed up their rods" (Exod. 7:10-12). Moses retained his identification with the snake as he led the tribes through the wilderness toward a concept of themselves as uniquely chosen by a single deity. However, Moses lost control of his following while on Mount Sinai to receive divine direction. Aaron, his brother, yielded to the pressure from the other faction, setting up a "molten calf: and they said, These be thy gods, O Israel, which brought thee up out of the land of Egypt" (Exod. 32:1-4). Upon his return, Moses "took the calf which they had made, and burnt it in the fire, and ground it to powder, and strawed it upon the water, and made the children of Israel drink of it" (Exod. 32:20). Later, having complained about the lack of bread and water, many Israelites died from the fatal bites of fiery serpents, sent as a divine response to this criticism: "And Moses made a serpent of brass, and put it upon a pole, and it came to pass, that if a serpent had bitten any man, when he beheld the serpent of brass, he lived" (Num. 21:7-9).

As the monotheistic definition of Yahweh developed, the conflict between factions continued to express itself in the symbols of worship. King Jeroboam, for example, "made two calves of gold, and said unto them, It is too much for you to go up to Jerusalem: behold thy gods, O Israel, which brought thee up out of the land of Egypt" (1 Kings 12:28). This dispute tended to coincide with the regional division of territory in which the Southern tribes (Judah)

> worshipped Yahweh under the symbol of the serpent, and the Northern tribes worshipped him under the symbol of the bull as his pedestal. Both kingdoms pointed back to events in the wilderness to defend their symbols, but the serpent symbol alone could in any sense be condoned because by tradition Moses was associated with such an emblem. (Joines 107)

Eventually King Hezekiah became convinced that allegiance to Yahweh would increase if there were no symbols whatever. Consequently, he "brake in pieces the serpent that Moses had made: for unto those days the children of Israel did burn incense to it" (2 Kings 18:4).

Familiar with this tradition, John the Apostle described why Christ needed to die by referring to the ancient image of redemption available to human beings who have sinned: "And as Moses lifted up the serpent in the wilderness, even so must the Son of man be lifted up: That whosoever believeth in him should not perish, but have eternal life" (John 3:14–15).

SNAKE AND BULL IN *BILLY BUDD*

Readers as familiar with this religious context as Melville was should not be surprised to find the character Melville represented by a snake coming into conflict with a character initially represented by a bull. The typical "Handsome Sailor," Melville indicates in the first paragraph of his tale, moves among his fellows "like Aldebaran among the lesser lights of his constellation." Editors Harrison Hayford and Merton M. Sealts, Jr. inform the reader that Aldebaran is the "'eye' of the constellation, Taurus, the Bull," preparing us for Melville's comment that the Handsome Sailor received adulation from his peers similar to that "which the Assyrian priests doubtless showed for their grand sculptured Bull when the faithful prostrated themselves." Billy is later addressed by his mates as "bully boy," and the narrator imagines that Claggart must have thought that Billy's spilling of his soup was "harmless, like the futile kick of a heifer."

For H. Bruce Franklin, Billy's association with this image indicates that Billy deserves to be worshipped. He points out that the Celtic god Budd, or Beli, is possibly the equivalent of Baal or Bel, who were "often represented by a sacred bull" which had to be sacrificed in order for salvation to occur. . . .

CLAGGART AND BILLY ARE NOT SIMPLE REPRESENTATIONS OF EVIL AND GOOD

Beyond allusions to the conflicts generated when people try to decide how omniscience is best portrayed—as bull or snake—Melville provides additional biblical references to deconstruct the dominant assumption that good can be readily distinguished from evil. Through repeated allusions Melville invites us to consider the possibility that Billy may not be totally innocent just as his serpentine villain may not be completely evil. . . .

To the extent that Billy changes during the course of the narrative he becomes more like Claggart because of Claggart. For although Billy remains a relatively static character, in his area of deficiency—knowledge—he grows through his experience with Claggart. Eventually Billy, unlike many critics, understands that his innocence is not total. He accepts guilt and expresses regret for his behavior (unpremeditated murder), though most of his past and future were outside his control: "I never bore malice against the master-at-arms. I am sorry that he is dead. I did not mean to kill him. Could I have used my tongue I would not have struck him." Like Claggart, Billy cannot escape his circumstances. Incapable of using language to resolve disputes, Billy resorts to force, a microcosmic reflection of the situation in which both he and Claggart find themselves—soldiers at war, professionally committed to the killing of other human beings who had been effectively reduced to personifications of evil.

In *Billy Budd* Melville makes repeated efforts to illustrate the absurdity of simplistic thinking. Taking a verbal jab at those who limit their search for truth to recorded documents, Melville includes an alternative account of events, as published in an official naval chronicle. Inverting the typical response to the story, Billy becomes depraved and Claggart the martyr: "'The enormity of the crime and the extreme depravity of the criminal appear the greater in view of the character of the victim, a middle-aged man respectable and discreet.'" Finally, readers are given the song of sailors who "instinctively felt that Billy was a sort of man as incapable of mutiny as of wilful murder." Though Billy is never accused of "wilful murder," the ballad, based on this illogical red herring lives on as an alternative equal to the official Navy version in its clarity, simplicity, and absurdity.

Thus Melville illustrates his major point by the way he tells his story, inviting readers to evaluate alternative interpretations of John Claggart. Admittedly, this is not tidy. "The symmetry of form attainable in pure fiction," writes Melville, "cannot so readily be achieved in a narration essentially having less to do with fable than with fact. Truth uncompromisingly told will always have its ragged edges." However, *Billy Budd* deals with fables as well as facts, and facts themselves are often influenced by the power of fables, as reported by human beings who perceive events according to the orthodox set of fables into which they happen to be born. Readers may judge whether this situation constitutes frustration or freedom, as ideas and images, like the skins of snakes, are shed and replaced in the human determination to escape the eternal ignorance of Eden.

Vere Represents Aristocratic Virtue

Thomas J. Scorza

In the last fifty years scholars have become increasingly vehement in either their celebration of or condemnation of Captain Vere. In this selection from his book *In the Time Before Steamships*, Melville scholar Thomas J. Scorza explores the character of Captain Vere by drawing attention to the context within which Melville introduces him. Although Melville was writing *Billy Budd* in America between 1886 and 1891, he sets the novel nearly one hundred years earlier on a British warship in the summer of 1797 during the French Revolutionary War. The threat of revolutionary ideas and actions, in addition to the fear of mutinies like the two that had occurred on British warships in the spring of 1797, made the summer of 1797 especially tense for the captain of a British warship. The historical admiral to whom Vere is compared is Lord Horatio Nelson, who distinguished himself countless times during the wars and who had been able to win back the allegiance of many mutineers. Nelson achieved a significant victory at the battle of Trafalgar, but died in the battle. For his heroic accomplishments he was called "the greatest sailor since our world began" by poet Alfred Lord Tennyson.

Melville introduces his fictional Captain Vere as a type of the "Great Sailor" like Nelson, but Melville also attributes to Vere other character traits, Scorza explains: Vere behaves like a born aristocrat, modest and self-effacing; he is an avid reader of histories, biographies, and philosophers who exercise common sense in their search for truth; and he is like the model statesman, whom Edmund Burke describes as one who must act prudently on his convictions for the good of the community he leads. Scorza sees Vere as an example of practical wisdom which will be tested severely in the crisis to come.

Excerpted from *In the Time Before Steamships: Billy Budd, The Limits of Politics and Modernity*, by Thomas J. Scorza (Dekalb: Northern Illinois University Press, 1979). Copyright © 1979 by Northern Illinois University Press. Reprinted with permission.

The description of the "handsome sailor" contained time and character references which served as background for the introduction of Billy Budd; in like manner, the novel's second major figure, Captain Vere, is introduced by references to a certain time and a certain phenomenal character. . . . In the case of Captain Vere, the background time reference is to the major political event of the modern age, the French Revolution, and the background character reference is to the Great Sailor, Lord Nelson; it is to be expected, thus, that the nature of Captain Vere will be revealed as it compares to and contrasts with the nature of the politically heroic figure of Lord Nelson. . . .

The narrator gives the historical background in a long paragraph in which a relationship is established between the mutiny within the British fleet and the war raging outside with revolutionary France:

> It was the summer of 1797. In the April of that year had occurred the commotion at Spithead followed in May by a second and yet more serious outbreak in the fleet at the Nore. The latter is known, and without exaggeration in the epithet, as "the Great Mutiny." It was indeed a demonstration more menacing to England than the contemporary manifestoes and conquering and proselyting armies of the French Directory. To the British Empire the Nore Mutiny was what a strike in the fire brigade would be to London threatened by general arson. . . .

The spring mutinies occurred at a time when Britain was threatened by the likes of "general arson" and "France in flames." While the French Directory and its "conquering and proselyting armies" constituted the direct threat to England, the mutinies endangered England's ability to meet that threat. The narrator does not present England as a merely reactionary force against revolutionary France, but rather as a "*free* conservative" power, displaying a flag of "founded law and *freedom* defined." That is, Britain is seen as a defender of a certain kind of freedom against "unbridled and unbounded revolt." The narrator's defense does not lead him to deny the fact that the mutinies grew out of very real "practical grievances." Later he notes that these grievances were such things as "shoddy cloth, rations not sound, or false in the measure," and especially, "impressment." But what might have been an agitation for practical reform was "ignited into irrational combustion," and what the government saw as the resulting "inadmissible" and "aggressively insolent" demands of the bluejackets "indicated—if the Red Flag did not sufficiently do so—what was the spirit animating the men." That is to say, the course which the sailors' discontent took revealed that their real grievances served also as vehicles for revolutionary agitation. . . .

ADMIRAL NELSON

The spring mutinies were finally suppressed, and the mutineers went on "to win a coronet for Nelson at the Nile, and the naval crown of crowns for him at Trafalgar." The subject of Nelson is thus raised in reference to this "plenary absolution" of the British mutineers, and a quasi-soteriological [salvific] relationship between the Great Sailor and the dangerous straits of the Empire is clearly suggested. . . .

Nelson embodied this dictate: "Personal prudence, even when dictated by quite other than selfish considerations, surely is no special virtue in a military man; while an excessive love of glory, impassioning a less burning impulse, the honest sense of duty, is the first." The glory and duty that moved Nelson at Trafalgar, the battle which absolved the sins of the mutineers, demanded a quasi-religious act, the implicitly deliberate act of consecrating the greatest victory with a sacrifice and thereby winning spiritual approval, forgiveness, and immortality for the victorious:

> At Trafalgar Nelson on the brink of opening the fight sat down and wrote his last brief will and testament. If under the presentiment of the most magnificent of all victories to be crowned by his own glorious death, a sort of priestly motive led him to dress his person in the jewelled vouchers of his own shining deeds; if thus to have adorned himself for the altar and the sacrifice were indeed vainglory, then affectation and fustian is each more heroic line in the great epics and dramas, since in such lines the poet but embodies in verse those exaltations of sentiment that a nature like Nelson, the opportunity being given, vitalizes into acts.

It is the *poet,* like the creator of *Billy Budd,* who embodies the glory of the Great Sailor in his verse. For this poet [Alfred Lord Tennyson], the Great Sailor exists as a paradigm of courage and honor, a paradigm by which allegiance is secured in the present and, perchance, in "the most magnificent of all victories," for all time. The end for which the Great Sailor acts is the preservation of the political community, and the actions he follows toward that end are scaled from those that concern individual units of the commonwealth to those that concern the whole's ultimate historical existence. At Trafalgar, Nelson dealt with the latter, but in "the same year with this story," he also showed his capacity for meeting a more particular crisis. Nelson was ordered from the *Captain* to the *Theseus,* "and for this reason: that the latter ship having newly arrived on the station from home, where it had taken part in the Great Mutiny, danger was apprehended from the temper of the men; and it was thought that an officer like Nelson was the one, not indeed to terrorize the crew into base subjection, but to win them, by force of his mere presence and heroic personality, back to an allegiance if not as enthusiastic as his own yet as true."

What Melville holds up as an example is the Great Sailor who acts for the common good. . . .

VERE: "A GREAT SAILOR"

Vere is to be compared with and contrasted to the Great Sailor as he acts in a situation in which "it was not unreasonable to apprehend some return of trouble sporadic or general." Vere's fate in this situation will reveal the limitations of another modern human type in the man-of-war world.

Because of the recent trouble, "precautionary vigilance was strained against relapse" aboard many British vessels. Indeed, in some instances, "the lieutenants assigned to batteries felt it incumbent on them . . . to stand with drawn swords behind the men working the guns." However, aboard H.M.S. *Bellipotent* "very little in the manner of the men and nothing obvious in the demeanor of the officers would have suggested to an ordinary observer that the Great Mutiny was a recent event." This lack of anxiety on the part of the officers and the concomitant calm of the men stem from one fact: "In their general bearing and conduct the commissioned officers of a warship naturally take their tone from the commander, that is if he have that ascendancy of character that ought to be his." Captain Vere's relationship to the officers and men is thus from the first pictured as exemplary: his "ascendancy of character" allows the *Bellipotent* to escape both abrasive "precautionary" tactics by the officers and overt hostility on the part of the crew. Where there was discontent and war, Captain Vere has brought calm and attention to duty. . . .

The narrator's description of Vere shows that his are the qualifications of a Great Sailor:

Captain the Honorable Edward Fairfax Vere, to give his full title, was a bachelor of forty or thereabouts, a sailor of distinc-
tion even in a time prolific of renowned seamen. Though al-
lied to the higher nobility, his advancement had not been
altogether owing to influences connected with that circumstance. He had seen much service, been in various engagements, always acquitting himself as an officer mindful of the
welfare of his men, but never tolerating an infraction of discipline; thoroughly versed in the science of his profession,
and intrepid to the verge of temerity, though never injudiciously so. For his gallantry in the West Indian waters as flag
lieutenant under Rodney in that admiral's crowning victory
over De Grasse, he was made a post captain.

Vere is thus a sailor of unquestioned ability, a nobleman
implicitly willing to use *some* influence to assure that his natural endowments won conventional stature, and a courageous disciplinarian. His intolerance of disciplinary infrac-
tions must be judged in the light of the description of the
situation aboard H.M.S. *Bellipotent:* like Nelson, Vere apparently is able to win allegiance and discipline without resorting to practices which "terrorize the crew into base subjection." Moreover, in a man-of-war world, discipline is an
absolute necessity; without discipline and regulations,
White-Jacket [a character in Melville's earlier novel, *White-
Jacket*] tells his readers, "a man-of-war's crew would be nothing but a mob." Thus, while Captain Vere's authority is plenary, his reign does not descend to the level of despotism.

VERE IS ALSO AN ARISTOCRAT

While Vere wears his rank well, both in the fleet and in society, he is capable of shedding the signs of his professional
stature and yet retaining his personal status. "Ashore, in the
garb of a civilian, scarce anyone would have taken him for a
sailor," and at quiet times at sea, "he was the most undemonstrative of men." In fact, his character is such that it
carries its own signs of social stature:

> Any landsman observing this gentleman not conspicuous by
> his stature and wearing no pronounced insignia, emerging
> from his cabin to the open deck, and noting the silent defer-
> ence of the officers retiring to leeward, might have taken
> him for the King's guest, a civilian aboard the King's ship,
> some highly honorable discreet envoy on his way to an im-
> portant post. But in fact this unobtrusiveness of demeanor
> may have proceeded from a certain unaffected modesty of
> manhood sometimes accompanying a resolute nature, a
> modesty evinced at all times not calling for pronounced ac-

tion, which shown in any rank of life suggests a virtue aristocratic in kind.

Vere is thus a nobleman, but one in a conventionally hierarchical society. Unlike the noble savage Mehevi in *Typee* [Melville's first novel], he is not simply one of "Nature's noblemen," but his abilities are nonetheless natural endowments. In Vere, nature and convention meet to distinguish one man from the mass of men. Whereas Billy's nobility is that of a "blood horse," Vere's is that of a born aristocrat. But Vere's standing as an aristocrat is more than just social and political. His popular nickname is "Starry Vere," and the narrator notes that this appellation is somewhat incongruous for "one who whatever his sterling qualities was without any brilliant ones." "Brilliant" and "Starry" in this sense are the opposites of "undemonstrative," "unobtrusive," and "unaffected"; the incongruity of the nickname lies in Vere's self-effacement and lack of ostentatiousness. His appellation is related to the fact that he "would at times betray a certain dreaminess of mood," and it was bestowed upon him at his return from his heroic West Indian cruise by a kinsman who had read these lines in Andrew Marvell's "Appleton House":

> This 'tis to have been from the first
> In a domestic heaven nursed,
> Under the discipline severe
> Of Fairfax and the starry Vere.

Vere's description thus adds an element that was absent in the portrait of Nelson as the Great Sailor. He is not only a man of courageous military spirit but also a man of a certain kind of distinguished intellect. His "starry" or celestial aspect, unlike Billy's and the "Handsome Sailor's," points not toward the figure of an animal, but toward the supposed height of humanity.

VERE IS AN INTELLECTUAL AND MODEL STATESMAN

"Aside from his qualities as a sea officer Captain Vere was an exceptional character." His exceptional quality was that of his mind:

> He had a marked leaning toward everything intellectual. He loved books, never going to sea without a newly replenished library, compact but of the best. . . . With nothing of that literary taste which less heeds the thing conveyed than the vehicle, his bias was toward those books to which every serious mind of superior order occupying any active post of author-

ity in the world naturally inclines: books treating of actual
men and events no matter of what era—history, biography,
and unconventional writers like Montaigne, who, free from
cant and convention, honestly and in the spirit of common
sense philosophize upon realities. . . .

As a reader, Captain Vere does not have a purely philosophic interest in truth, for as a person of authority, he must
act; in action, truth gives way to prudence. He is, in action, an
analogue of [Edmund] Burke's statesman, whose thought and
effort aim only at "the concrete and limited good of the particular community which he has to govern, and not the good
of man in the abstract." His historical studies serve as a
ground for the political principle upon which he acts, and just
as he stands above his fellow officers by reason of his "bookish" nature, he stands above his intellectual contemporaries
by reason of his "disinterested" but practical convictions:

> In this line of reading he found confirmation of his own more
> reserved thoughts—confirmation which he had vainly sought
> in social converse, so that as touching most fundamental top-
> ics, there had got to be established in him some positive con-
> victions which he forefelt would abide in him essentially un-
> modified so long as his intelligent part remained unimpaired.
> In view of the troubled period in which his lot was cast, this
> was well for him. His settled convictions were as a dike
> against those invading waters of novel opinion social, politi-
> cal, and otherwise, which carried away as in a torrent no few
> minds in those days, minds by nature not inferior to his own.
> While other members of that aristocracy to which by birth he
> belonged were incensed at the innovators mainly because
> their theories were inimical to the privileged classes, Captain
> Vere disinterestedly opposed them not alone because they
> seemed to him insusceptible of embodiment in lasting insti-
> tutions, but at war with the peace of the world and the true
> welfare of mankind.

As Vere is introduced, therefore, the reader meets a man
who has arrived at a state of equilibrium: his political beliefs
as a Burkean conservative have established a *modus vivendi*
[way of living, a practical compromise] with his unconventional inclination to "philosophize upon realities." His "settled convictions" against novel theories derive from his
practical belief in the human need for "lasting institutions"
and his traditionalist notion of "the true welfare of mankind." He is distinguished from both the "innovators" and
the self-interested "aristocrats," positioning himself, with
practical truth, in the middle. As ruler of the *Bellipotent,* he

seems to be the epitome of the Burkean politician, a "philosopher in action." As captain and king of a ship of state, he seems to have achieved that coincidence of philosophy and rule which might promise to alleviate human or political ills. His ship is apparently ruled by practical wisdom as it prepares for war and victory.

Melville Condemns the Tyrannical Vere

H. Bruce Franklin

In this selection from his article, "From Empire to
Empire: *Billy Budd, Sailor*," Rutgers University professor of English and American literature H. Bruce
Franklin, asserts that *Billy Budd* is "fundamentally
unambiguous." He claims that Melville clearly condemns Vere and the British imperialism which he
serves. Furthermore, Franklin explains that Melville
is warning his own American contemporaries
against similar budding imperialist desires. Drawing
evidence from Melville's life, earlier works (especially the novel *White-Jacket*), current research, and
his own reading of the novel, Franklin presents
twenty-two points on which he grounds his argument for Melville's condemnation of Captain Vere.

In addition to other articles on *Billy Budd*, Franklin has
published several books. The most recent are *Prison Literature in America* and *Robert A. Heinlein: America as Science
Fiction*.

The priceless currency of Melville's tale is implicitly acknowledged by the great debate raging since 1950 about its
meaning. But the time has come for us to move beyond this
debate, for it tells us far more about our epoch and about the
terrifying values of those who misread the story, than it does
about Melville's meaning, which is fundamentally unambiguous. This is not to deny the profundity or the complexity or the richness of the story. Quite the contrary, for the
murky fog of supposed ambiguity—generated mainly by the
confusion (or worse) of some academics—has tended to ob-
scure the luminous insights dramatized by *Billy Budd* and
thus to deprive us of its guiding light as we try to steer out of
the deadly straits toward which Melville saw us heading.

One of the more appalling symptoms of our predicament is the spectacle of some modern readers, apparently intelligent, humane, learned, and well-intentioned, fulfilling the prophecy of the story by exalting precisely the conduct and values against which Melville desperately warns. The fact that such people can argue that Captain Vere incarnates 'virtue' or Melville's one authentic 'hero' merely displays the treacherous, insidious character of some of the ethical norms of our society and the function of Vere's intellectual counterparts today. . . .

THE CASE AGAINST VERE

(1) The story, not entitled *Edward Vere, Captain,* glorifies Vere's victim, *Billy Budd, Sailor,* designated 'the main figure' of a tale in which he appears from beginning to end. Vere, a late addition in the composition, is not even mentioned in seventeen out of the thirty chapters.

(2) Budd is one of three embodiments of the truly heroic figure, 'the Handsome Sailor', who appears first in the dedication to Jack Chase, Melville's actual shipmate and Handsome Sailor virtually deified in *White-Jacket,* and then in the colossal opening image of the Black African, a godlike man, combining 'strength and beauty', the 'champion' of his shipmates, workers of 'such an assortment of tribes and complexions' that they could serve as the 'Representatives of the Human Race'.

(3) To think that Melville at all condones Vere's action one must divorce the story from Melville's actual life as a foretopman on a man-of-war, recalled not only in the dedication to Jack Chase but also in the overtly autobiographical details woven into the narrative. For example, if Billy Budd must be hanged, then Jack Chase should also have been hanged, for he openly and with full intent defied his captain and the Articles of War, deserting his ship to fight for Peruvian independence—because of his devotion to 'the Rights of Man'. Yet even the vicious Captain Claret has enough sense to give him no harsher punishment than a mild verbal rebuke. In Melville's imagination the hanging of the Handsome Sailor is no mere metaphor. Would he have admired or been ambiguous about a captain who executed another incarnation of Jack Chase?

(4) Those who argue that *Billy Budd* is the product of 'an old man's quiet conservatism' and that Melville in his 'old

age' here renounces his earlier values should re-read *John Marr and Other Sailors,* published in 1888, including poems like 'Bridegroom Dick', in which 'the formidable Finn' threatens officers and attacks the Master-at-arms, only to be released with a mere threat of a flogging by the 'magnanimous' captain.

(5) Vere explicitly repudiates the Rights of Man, the dictates of conscience, nature, and any law or truth higher than the most ruthless code of military justice, a code denounced systematically by Melville in chapter after chapter of *White-Jacket* as 'bloodthirsty' and 'tyrannical'. For example, in Chapter 71 he brands the American Articles of War a detestable importation 'even from Britain, whose laws we Americans hurled off as tyrannical, and yet retained the most tyrannical of all'. . . .

(6) Throughout Melville's works, his loathing of war and imperialism is expressed in key images that recur in *Billy Budd.* This central point is explored in depth in Joyce Adler's marvellous book, *War in Melville's Imagination.*

(7) Vere orders the atrocity most passionately excoriated in *White-Jacket,* flogging a sailor—for precisely the same offence for which White Jacket himself was sentenced to be flogged. Billy's thoughts on witnessing this flogging are identical to Melville's recorded thoughts on witnessing his first flogging. White Jacket was prepared to murder his captain, if necessary, to preserve his humanity against this barbarous practice, which Melville himself helped stop in the U.S. Navy. White Jacket is saved only by the personal intervention of Jack Chase.

(8) Vere demands of his officers and himself that 'the heart', 'the feminine in man', 'must here be ruled out' so that they can kill Budd. But Melville had always chosen the heart. As he put it in his famous 1851 letter to Hawthorne: 'I stand for the heart. To the dogs with the head!' This allegiance is repledged throughout *Billy Budd,* from the very words of dedication to Jack Chase: 'that great heart'.

(9) In order to effect his will and carry out his snap judgement that he must hang Billy, Vere himself actually must violate the very code which he claims to be enforcing. Vere had no authority to administer a punishment greater than twelve lashes, his drumhead court is illegal, and a case such as this had to be submitted to higher levels.

(10) Some attribute this to Melville's alleged ignorance of

the British naval code of the period, though he did research on this question while working on the story. However, Vere's own officers are aware of what the code does dictate, that they are supposed to 'postpone further action' in such a case until 'they rejoin the squadron, and then refer it to the admiral', and they, as well as other officers later, believe that Vere acts improperly.

(11) Vere's procedures are compared to those of 'Peter the Barbarian', the infamous Russian czar.

(12) Melville compares Vere's procedures with the hanging of three men on the U.S. brig *Somers,* which he had unequivocally denounced (see, for example, *White-Jacket,* Chs. 70 and 72), though in that case there was some evidence of a planned mutiny.

(13) Vere's action, and his entire argument to his drumhead court, is based on a fear of an imminent mutiny. But we readers of this 'Inside Narrative' never see the faintest hint of any such possibility. Discipline is only breached *after* Billy's execution.

(14) Vere's drumhead court, all British naval officers, all familiar with the recent mutinies in the British navy as well as the situation on the *Bellipotent,* each hand-picked by Vere himself as most likely to support his prejudgement, do not agree to have Billy hanged until Vere manipulates, tricks, and coerces them with a combination of his authority over them, his better-trained intellect, and rhetoric.

(15) Although Vere's verbal adroitness (the opposite of Billy's tongue-tied innocence) overwhelms this trio of naval officers, to trained students of rhetoric his devious methods are blatantly specious. . . .

(16) The core of Vere's argument is that 'Nature', 'the heart', and 'the conscience' must all be subordinated to the particular order embodied by the British King and British Empire. This is the king and empire from which America had just won its freedom.

(17) This very king was a notorious madman. Vere's own argument inadvertently recalls that one of George III's most famous symptoms of insanity was his obsession with making buttons, giving him the sobriquet of 'The Button Maker': 'But do these buttons that we wear attest that our allegiance is to Nature? No, to the King' (267–68).

(18) On one hand, this displays what James Farnham has called Vere's 'existential failure': 'Vere hides inside his uni-

form. . . . He reverts to a clothes philosophy, to the pleasing untruth that the clothes, in this instance the gold buttons on an officer's uniform, define the man. . . .'

(19) It also points to the horrendous fallacy in Vere's historical position. As Edgar Dryden has demonstrated at length, 'The appalling truth of *Billy Budd* is not that innocence must be sacrificed to maintain the order of the world, but rather that innocence is destroyed by the forces of chaos and darkness masquerading as "measured forms".'

(20) Except for his dying murmur of 'Billy Budd, Billy Budd', Vere's last quoted words sum up the philosophy he embodies: '"With mankind," he would say, "forms, measured forms, are everything; and that is the import couched in the story of Orpheus with his lyre spellbinding the wild denizens of the wood"'. This grotesquely perverted view of poetry, music, imagination, and beauty is contradicted on every level—aesthetic, ontological, and ethical—by the form and content of *Billy Budd, Sailor.*

(21) These 'forms, measured forms' are immediately repudiated by the narrator's dismissal of 'the symmetry of form attainable in pure fiction'.

(22) Those ignorant sailors—whom Vere so deeply fears and so disdains that he hangs 'an angel of God' to keep them in line—have the last word. The final words of the tale are in the formless art of a 'rude' ballad, made by the 'tarry hand' of 'another foretopman'—obviously Melville himself, who had, like Budd, been a foretopman. . . .

VERE'S POSITIVE QUALITIES HEIGHTEN THE HORROR OF HIS DECISIONS

Vere does have many positive qualities, but these serve to strengthen Melville's case against the system he serves and to heighten the emotional horrors of his decision. If he were an especially tyrannical, unjust, irrational, brutal, or ignorant captain, his act could be ascribed to his personal character rather than to the military and imperialist institution of which he is, by his own argument, merely an officer.

Only two men in the ship are 'intellectually capable of adequately appreciating the moral phenomenon presented in Billy Budd'. One is Claggart, who 'could even have loved Billy'. The other is Vere, whose wilful sacrifice of the transcendent being he recognizes as 'an angel of god' becomes an overwhelming heart-rending loss of freedom, love, and human possibilities. If Vere were a mere stage villain, his act would evoke more anger than anguish. But to argue that therefore Melville must condone or admire his act is tantamount to saying that Shakespeare condones or admires Othello's murder of Desdemona, an act also made more appalling because of the finer qualities of the murderer.

There is only one ambiguity about Vere: is he sane or mad? Insofar as the story focuses on Vere, it is the study of an apparently rational, humane man who can argue with learning, calm, and some plausibility that the most ethical course of action is to kill the most innocent and beloved person in your world to preserve the military law and order necessary for monarchy and empire. . . .

A Warning Against Militarism and Imperialism

The forces served by Captain Vere did indeed triumph over the hero of *The Rights of Man.* The British Empire, temporarily set back by the American revolution, was soon moving ahead full speed, in tides of blood, everywhere on the planet, using its almost total hegemony over the seas to extend its rule to over a quarter of the world's population, mostly non-white.

While feudalism was being replaced by capitalism, and Vere's aristocratic class, with its ancient blood lines, was being replaced by men like Claggart, rising by their wits and cunning from unknown origins to the key places of power, the industrial revolution was transforming mercantile capitalism into industrial capitalism. Industrial capitalism demanded colonies and provided the means to acquire them: steamships, instantaneous communication, new weapons of unprecedented destructive power, armies of desperate unemployed men.

Let us not forget that Melville first made his mark as one of the boldest anti-imperialist writers of the century. His outrage focused on the islands of the Pacific, where 'the civilized white man', whom he brands 'the most ferocious animal on the face of the earth', was using warships and missionaries to enslave the so-called 'savages' and 'barbarians'. All this is compressed into the passages after Billy is equated with 'those so-called barbarian' peoples who 'stand nearer to unadulterate Nature'. He receives the Christian chaplain of the *Bellipotent* just as missionaries were 're-ceived long ago on tropic isles by any superior *savage,* so called—a Tahitian, say. . . .' In a stunning comparison that foreshadows the opening section of [Joseph] Conrad's *Heart of Darkness,* Melville reminds the English imperialists (and their American descendants) that their ancestors were once treated as they now treat such illiterate 'barbarians' as common sailors and Pacific islanders:

> And, as elsewhere said, a barbarian Billy radically was—as much so, for all the costume, as his countrymen the British captives, living trophies, made to march in the Roman triumph of Germanicus. Quite as much so as those later barbarians, young men probably, and picked specimens among the earlier British converts to Christianity, at least nominally such, taken to Rome (as today converts from lesser isles of the sea may be taken to London). . . .

I am not implying that *Billy Budd* is some kind of anti-British or jingoistic diatribe. For *Billy Budd* was written just as America was about to transform into a world empire resembling the British empire against which it had rebelled. The story foresees the consequences of unbridled militarism and imperialism, which obliterate the rights of man not only in the colonized lands but also among the people forced to do the fighting and colonizing. By going a century into the past to explore the consequences of the triumph of militarism and imperialism in England, it foreshadows the century of the future, with the consequences of the triumph of militarism and imperialism in America.

Captain Vere: Nineteenth-Century Tragic Hero

Richard A. Hocks

University of Missouri professor Richard A. Hocks
considers Captain Vere a nineteenth-century tragic
hero because he wrestles with the central dilemma
in nineteenth-century American letters: romantic
faith in intuition versus realistic focus on material-
ism and utilitarianism. Hocks sees Vere as a romantic to the degree that he is dreamy, contemplative,
and a reader who has arrived at certain fundamental
convictions based on intuited principles. Vere's particular convictions are presented in the first part of
his argument to the officers he has appointed to
judge Billy's case, Hocks explains. Since the officers
depend upon their intuitive assurance of Billy's innocence, Vere's argument fails. Vere uses the utilitarian
approach in the second part of his argument, and
thereby convinces his officers to condemn Billy to
death. Hocks sees Vere's use of the utilitarian argument as his tragic error. Not only does Vere undermine his own romantic principles by using this utilitarian approach, but he also convinces his officers to
override their intuitive convictions in the interest of
self-preservation. Melville knew that utilitarian
thought did in fact succeed romantic idealism in
nineteenth-century American letters and policy.
Ironically, utilitarianism, the root of modern democratic institutions, is the very approach that kills
such innocent heroes as Billy Budd.

Richard A. Hocks is a noted American literature scholar
whose books include *Henry James: A Study of the Short
Fiction* and *Henry James and Pragmatic Thought.* He is
also co-editor of the Norton Critical Edition of James's *The
Wings of the Dove.*

Excerpted from "Melville and 'The Rise of Realism': The Dilemma of History in *Billy
Budd,*" by Richard A. Hocks, *American Literary Realism,* Winter 1994. Copyright © 1994
by the Department of English, The University of New Mexico. Reprinted with permission.

In recent decades the scholarship of *Billy Budd* has greatly emphasized the role and moral status of Captain Vere. This was justified by Hayford and Sealts, although the focal swing to Vere had already begun before the publication of their work; as Hershel Parker too perfunctorily has said very recently: "At the end of the 1950s, then, interpretation was polarized—Vere was good and Melville liked him (as any decent person would).". . .

Vere is, certainly, the key to *Billy Budd.* His emergence in the third compositional phase is what gives the work its true dialectic, because Vere's presence brings explicitly into the forefront the issue of time and history, the very issue which, so to speak, gave birth to him as the novel's eventual center. This is immediately apparent in the fact that he is not a protagonist with mysterious origins, but is instead rooted in history by his name and family. Furthermore, if we keep in mind Melville's aims for a classical tragedy together with Aristotle's view that philosophy provides the idea without the event, history the event without the idea, and tragedy the idea as event, then perhaps Captain Vere provides *Billy Budd* with the event. From his vantage point in 1890 Melville reminds the reader again and again that this is 1797, following upon the upheaval of the French Revolution, and seems to presage the disintegration of the Western society intact since the Middle Ages: "Reasonable discontent growing out of practical grievances in the fleet had been ignited into irrational combustion as by live cinders blown across the Channel from France in flames."

A CHARACTER TRAGICALLY DIVIDED

Unlike Billy and Claggart, then, Vere is of a real time and place. He is historical both by his name and by his conscious view of mankind and society. An aristocrat and a descendant of the Fairfax family, Melville significantly introduces him to the reader as "Captain the Honorable Edward Fairfax Vere." Perhaps Melville's reason for making Vere a Fairfax was his recollection of the tense, ambivalent role in English history of General Fairfax, commander in chief of the army of parliament against Charles I in the English Civil War. In the seventeenth-century conflict Fairfax emerges as a figure caught tragically in the middle—an aristocrat with compassion and sympathy for his king, yet persuaded by principle to cast his lot, reluctantly, with the roundheads. Melville's captain thus suggests a counter-portrait: a man in authority with compassion and sympathy for the individual representing the new order, but against whom he reluctantly acts from principle. . . .

Vere is in fact the only one of the three who emerges as a character, tragic or otherwise, instead of an emblem. He seems a character primarily because he alone articulates at any length the central issues and conflicts of the narrative—the claims of nature, compassion, heavenly justice; and the counter-claims of law, order, duty, and necessity. Since he is, then, our only real candidate for a tragic hero in a "nineteenth-century version of classical tragedy," let me suggest the possibility of his flaw and relate it to the matters discussed in this essay.

VERE'S DREAMY, CONTEMPLATIVE CHARACTER

Vere is first presented to us in Chapters Six and Seven. In the first of these chapters we learn of his character and temperament, and in the second of his political and moral philosophy. We learn, for example, of his appellation "starry Vere," owing to "a certain dreaminess of mood," and evidenced in his tendency to "absently gaze off at the blank sea"; evidenced, too, is what is called by his fellow officers "a queer streak of the pedantic."

> Some apparent ground there was for this sort of confidential criticism; since . . . in illustrating of any point touching the stirring personages and events of the time he would be as apt to cite some historic character or incident from antiquity as he would be to cite from the moderns. He seemed unmindful of the circumstance that to his bluff company such remote allusions, however pertinent they might really be, were altogether alien to men whose reading was mainly confined to the journals. But considerateness in such matters is not easy to natures constituted like Captain Vere's.

He is fundamentally a scholar in disposition, if not in practice or circumstance. Melville clarifies this by pointing out that in civilian dress no one would take him for a sailor, and might even have been mistaken for a guest aboard the King's ship rather than its captain. Thus it is primarily his external paraphernalia which Melville associates with his role as sea captain, while it is his dreaminess and contemplation, separating him by temperament and "discourse" from his peers, which represent the essential inner man. His world view, the primary subject of Chapter Seven, proceeds from the *inner* man:

> He had a marked leaning toward everything intellectual. He
> loved books, never going to sea without a newly replenished
> library, compact but of the best . . . . In this line of reading
> [writers free from cant, like Montaigne] he found confirma-
> tion of his own more reserved thoughts—confirmation which
> he had vainly sought in social converse, so that as touching
> most fundamental topics, there had got to be established in
> him some positive convictions which he forefelt would abide
> in him essentially unmodified. . . . His settled convictions
> were as a dike against those invading waters of novel opinion
> social, political, and otherwise, which carried away as in a
> torrent no few minds in those days, minds by nature not in-
> ferior to his own.

All of this points to a mentality which is opposed in the very
nexus of its thought to the Utilitarian school Melville associates with the growth of his century after the days of Nelson. . . .

VERE'S ARGUMENT AT THE TRIAL

We go therefore to Vere's conduct at the trial for evidence of
his error or tragic flaw, since the trial amounts to an address
by him to the three junior officers who make up the drumhead court, an address noteworthy for its being the only sus-
tained articulation of the central moral and philosophical
issues by anyone other than the author/narrator. In my judgment, the text of this speech warrants our dividing it into two
parts, or phases: the first, a primarily speculative argument
based on fundamental convictions derived from innate principles and abstract thought; the second, a practical argument
based primarily on more immediate, utilitarian considerations. Here is the center of his argument during the first part:

> How can we adjudge to summary and shameful death a fel-
> low creature innocent before God, and whom we feel to be
> so?—Does that state it aright? You sign sad assent. . . . It is Na-
> ture. But do these buttons that we wear attest that our alle-
> giance is to Nature? No, to the King. Though the ocean, which
> is inviolate Nature primeval, though this be the element
> where we move and have our being as sailors, yet as the
> King's officers lies our duty in a sphere correspondingly nat-
> ural? So little is that true, that in receiving our commissions
> we in the most important regards ceased to be natural free
> agents. . . . If our judgments approve the war, that is but co-
> incidence. So in other particulars. So now. For suppose con-
> demnation to follow these present proceedings. Would it be
> so much we ourselves that would condemn as it would be
> martial law operating through us.

It is important to recognize that, although Vere is trying to
argue, as he says, not as "casuist" or "moralist" but with a

"case practical," he still exhibits his anti-Benthamite [anti-utilitarian, romantic] mentality by his intellectual perspective and discourse. There is a philosophical division here which parallels the dramatic dividedness of mind in the court. The officers are of course troubled because they intuit Billy's innocence. Vere's division of mind is more complicated, since he not only shares with them the realization of Billy's innocence but is convinced—along with Melville's narrator—that "the unhappy event could not have happened at a worse juncture . . . close on the heels of the suppressed insurrections." Vere's division of mind is complicated furthermore by the recognition that he must "demonstrate certain principles that were axioms to himself" to "men not intellectually mature.". . .

Vere's natural and quick intellectual jump from "fellow human being" to "Nature"—even though to insist that duty must take precedence over nature—is the demonstrable cast of his mind. And that is why the officers fail as yet to be convinced by his argument: "Here the three men moved in their seats, less convinced than agitated by the course of an argument troubling but the more the spontaneous conflict within. Perceiving which, the speaker paused for a moment; then abruptly changing his tone, went on."

THE SECOND PHASE OF VERE'S ARGUMENT

At this juncture Captain Vere, in his attempt to communicate his a priori convictions (settled as a dike) to men beneath his level of understanding, comes to "modify" considerably more than just his "tone":

> "Gentlemen . . . consider the consequences of such clemency. The people . . . have native sense; most of them are familiar with our naval usage and tradition; and how would they take it? . . . No, to the people the foretopman's deed . . . will be plain homicide committed in a flagrant act of mutiny. What penalty for that should follow, they know. But it does not follow. *Why?* they will ruminate. You know what sailors are. Will they not revert to the recent outbreak at the Nore? Ay. They know the well-founded alarm—the panic it struck throughout England. Your clement sentence they would account pusillanimous. They would think that we flinch, that we are afraid of them—afraid of practicing of a lawful rigor singularly demanded at this juncture, lest it should provoke new troubles."

This second "phase" of Vere's argument, which lacks that sense of "antiquity" we have come to expect from him (note how much closer to it reads the previous passage), is what persuades the court to condemn. And Melville's narrator underscores this: ". . . it is not improbable that even such of his words as were not without influence over them, less came home to them than his closing appeal to their instincts as sea officers: in the forethought he threw out as to the practical consequences to discipline."

Captain Vere has found the appropriate "discourse" for his fellow officers by resorting to the pragmatist's argument. His address has undergone its crucial "modifications" by virtue of needing to persuade the court of his fixed principles. We are watching, in short, the very transformation of history: Captain Vere has been forced to employ the resources of the utilitarian argument in order to preserve from his perspective in 1797 a world view which, as Melville knew from his perspective in 1890, was to run counter to the actual direction of subsequent history; a direction whose philosophical roots were in Utilitarian thought and its complement, the growth of democratic institutions. Therefore Captain Vere emerges as the most profound demonstration in *Billy Budd* of the actual and inevitable course of that history in the very formulation by which he would have asserted and implemented an alternative history. Perhaps only in this way could Melville give to his work an equivalence to the tragic flaw and irony, one which historically could "hold the Present at its worth without being inappreciative of the Past."

CHAPTER 2

Competing Interpretations of *Billy Budd*

Melville's Testament of Acceptance

E.L. Grant Watson

E.L. Grant Watson has been credited with beginning the "testament of acceptance" theory, a reading of *Billy Budd* which asserts Billy's acceptance of impressment and later, death, Vere's acceptance of responsibility, and Melville's acceptance of evil as the necessary opposite of good. In this selection, Watson presents his position. He quotes from the first transcription of *Billy Budd*, made by Raymond Weaver in 1924, in which the British warship is identified as the *Indomitable* rather than the *Bellipotent*, which is the ship's name in the 1962 standard transcription.

E.L. Grant Watson was a practicing psychotherapist who published articles on Melville's novels *Pierre* and *Moby-Dick*, as well as on *Billy Budd*. He is also author of *The Mystery of Physical Life*, and in 1990 Dorothy Green collected his work in *Descent of Spirit: Writings of E.L. Grant Watson*.

The story [*Billy Budd*] develops simply, always unhurried, yet never lagging. Each character is described with the patience which the complex intention of the theme demands—the color of the eyes, the clothes, the complexion, the color of the skin, of the blood under the skin, the past, the present—these are hints at a deep and solemn purpose, one no less ambitious than to portray those ambiguities of good and evil as the mutually dependent opposites, between which the world of realization finds its being. . . .

Melville called his story "an inside narrative," and though it deals with events stirring and exciting enough in themselves, it is yet more exciting because it deals with the relation of those principles which constitute life itself. A simple-mindedness unaffected by the shadow of doubt, a divine innocence and courage, which might suggest a Christ not

yet conscious of His divinity, and a malice which has lost itself in the unconscious depths of mania—the very mystery
of iniquity—these opposites here meet, and find their des-
tiny. But Melville's theme is even larger. All the grim setting
of the world is in the battleship *Indomitable;* war and threatened mutiny are the conditions of her existence. Injustice
and inhumanity are implicit, yet Captain Vere, her commander, is the man who obeys the law, and yet understands the
truth of the spirit. It is significant of Melville's development
since the writing of *Moby-Dick* and *Pierre,* that he should
create this naval captain—wholly pledged to the unnatural-
ness of the law, but sufficiently touched, at the same time, by
the divine difference from ordinary sanity (he goes by the
nick-name of "Starry Vere"), as to live the truth *within* the
law, and yet, in the cruel process of that very obedience, to
redeem an innocent man from the bitterness of death imposed by the same law. A very different ending this from the
despairing acts of dissolution which mark the conclusions of
the three earlier books: *Mardi, Moby-Dick,* and *Pierre.*

THE CHARACTERS' QUALITIES OF ACCEPTANCE

Melville is no longer a rebel. It should be noted that Billy
Budd has not, even under the severest provocation, any element of rebellion in him; he is too free a soul to need a quality which is a virtue only in slaves. His nature spontaneously
accepts whatever may befall. When impressed from the
merchant-ship, the *Rights of Man,* he makes no demur to
the visiting lieutenant's order to get ready his things for
trans-shipment. The crew of the merchant-ship are surprised and reproachful at his uncomplaining acquiescence.
Once aboard the battleship, the young sailor begins to look
around for the advantages of chance and adventure. Such
simple power to accept gives him the buoyancy to override
troubles and irritations which would check inferior natures.

Yet his complete unconsciousness of the attraction, and
consequent repulsion, that his youthful beauty and unso-
phisticated good-fellowship exercise on Claggart, make it
only easier for these qualities to turn envy into hatred. His
very virtue makes him the target for the shaft of evil, and his
quality of acceptance provokes to action its complementary
opposite, the sense of frustration that can not bear the consciousness of itself, and so has to find escape in mania. Thus
there develops the conflict between unconscious virtue (not

even aware of its loss of Eden and unsuspecting of the presence of evil) and the bitter perversion of love which finds its
only solace in destruction.

And not only Billy Budd is marked by this supreme quality of acceptance. Captain Vere, also, possesses it, but with
full consciousness, and weighted with the responsibility of
understanding the natural naturalness of man's volition and
the unnatural naturalness of the law. In the summing up at
the drum-head court-martial of the case for the law against
the innocent man, he said:

> Now can we adjudge to summary and shameful death a fel-
> low-creature innocent before God, and whom we feel to be
> so?—Does that state it right? You sign sad assent. Well, I too
> feel the full force of that. It is Nature. But do these buttons that
> we wear attest that our allegiance is to Nature? No, to the
> King. Though the ocean, which is inviolate Nature primeval,
> though this be the element where we move and have our be-
> ing as sailors, yet as the King's officers lies our duty in a
> sphere correspondingly natural? . . . We fight at command. If
> our judgements approve the war, that is but coincidence. So
> in other particulars. So now, would it be not so much our-
> selves that would condemn as it would be martial law oper-
> ating through us? For that law and the rigour of it, we are not
> responsible. Our vowed responsibility is in this: That how-
> ever pitilessly that law may operate, we nevertheless adhere
> to it and administer it.

In Captain Vere we find a figure which may interestingly be
compared to Pontius Pilate. Like Pilate, he condemns the just
man to a shameful death, knowing him to be innocent, but,
unlike Pilate, he does not wash his hands, but manfully assumes the full responsibility, and in such a way as to take
the half, if not more than the half, of the bitterness of the execution upon himself. We are given to suppose that there is
an affinity, a spiritual understanding between Captain Vere
and Billy Budd, and it is even suggested that in their partial
and separate existences they contribute two essential por-
tions of that larger spirit which is man. . . .

AN IMAGE OF UNITY

For his suggestive use of words, and the special values he
gives them, and the large implication he can in this way
compress into a sentence, the passage which tells how Billy
Budd was hanged from the main yard-arm of the battle-ship
Indomitable is a good example:

> Billy stood facing aft. At the penultimate moment, his words,

his only ones, words wholly unobstructed in the utterance, were these—"God bless Captain Vere!" Syllables so unantici- pated coming from one with the ignominious hemp about his neck—a conventional felon's benediction directed aft to- wards the quarters of honour; syllables, too, delivered in the clear melody of a singing bird on the point of launching from the twig, had a phenomenal effect, not unenhanced by the rare personal beauty of the young sailor, spiritualised now through late experiences so poignantly profound.

Without volition, as it were, as if indeed the ship's populace were the vehicles of some vocal current-electric, with one voice, from alow and aloft, came a resonate echo—"God bless Captain Vere!" And yet at that instant Billy alone must have been in their hearts, even as he was in their eyes.

At the pronounced words and the spontaneous echo that vo- luminously rebounded them, Captain Vere, either through stoic self-control or a sort of momentary paralysis induced by emotional shock, stood erectly rigid as a musket in the ship- armourer's rack.

The hull, deliberately recovering from the periodic roll to lee- ward, was just regaining an even keel, when the last signal, the preconcerted dumb one, was given. At the same moment it chanced that the vapoury fleece hanging low in the east, was shot through with a soft glory as of the fleece of the Lamb of God seen in mystical vision, and simultaneously therewith, watched by the wedged mass of upturned faces, Billy ascended; and ascending, took the full rose of the dawn.

In the pinioned figure, arrived at the yard-end, to the wonder of all, no motion was apparent save that created by the slow roll of the hull, in moderate weather so majestic in a great ship heavy-cannoned.

Here is Melville at his very best, at his deepest, most poetic, and therefore at his most concentrated, most conscious. Every image has its significant implication: the very roll of the heavily-cannoned ship so majestic in moderate weather—the musket in the ship-armourer's rack; and Billy's last words are the triumphant seal of his acceptance, and they are more than that, for in this supreme passage a communion between per- sonality at its purest, most-God-given form, and character, hard-hammered from the imperfect material of life on the battleship *Indomitable,* is here suggested, and one feels that the souls of Captain Vere and Billy are at that moment strangely one.

Billy Budd: Testament of Resistance

Phil Withim

Professor Phil Withim takes issue with the view that Melville's work can be read as a testament of acceptance. Instead, he sees in *Billy Budd* a call to resist evil, tyranny, and perverted reasoning. In this selection, Withim focuses on the narrator's description of Vere, and he notes the possibility that it can be read ironically. The narrator may not be praising Vere as a reader but may be hinting that Vere reads only books which reinforce his own opinions. Vere's argument for strict adherence to the law may also be understood as a criticism of Vere, Withim explains, because Melville is consistently opposed to strict adherence to cruel and unjust laws. Comparisons of Vere, Admiral Nelson, and Claggart reveal Vere to be less heroic than Nelson and more like the evil Claggart than at first appears. The work is not a straightforward call to rebellion against tyranny, Withim explains; instead, it encourages resistance to evil by showing the consequences of unresisting acceptance of authority.

Phil Withim is also co-author of *The Binding of Proteus: Perspectives of Myth and the Literary Process.*

When E.L.G. Watson wrote his famous article, "Melville's Testament of Acceptance," he made no attempt to prove his view. All he attempted, all he achieved, was to suggest a way of looking at the story. "Melville," said Watson, "is no longer a rebel." He has come to accept the presence of evil, and he has ceased to blame God for its existence. Other critics began to write on *Billy Budd* in the same vein. Their positions varied somewhat, but the tenor, the direction of the viewpoint was always the same: Melville had mellowed, he was resigned, as [F. Barron] Freeman says, to the recognition of necessity. In F.O. Matthiessen's words, "He has come to respect necessity. . . . Melville could now face incongruity; he could accept the existence of both good and evil. . . ." Or as Willard Thorp remarks, "In the end Melville called the truce."

There was, however, some dissent; both Alfred Kazin and Richard Chase indicated dissatisfaction with the "testament of acceptance" theory. In 1950 Joseph Schiffman, in an article which reviewed all these interpretations as well as those of [Lewis] Mumford, [Charles] Weir, and [William Ellery] Sedgwick, put forth a suggestion, which he credited to Gay Wilson Allen, "that *Billy Budd* might best be understood as a work of irony." Since this article appeared, a number of other critics have also objected to the "testament of acceptance" theory or have supported an ironic interpretation; sometimes they have done both.

This paper is another step in this same direction. It accepts the point of view that *Billy Budd* was written in a basically ironic style; it will attempt to establish a thesis in harmony with all of the parts of the story and to demonstrate that the "testament of acceptance" theory is essentially self-contradictory.

The body of the story is concerned with the relationships of three men: Billy Budd, John Claggart, and Captain Vere. Whatever arguments may rage concerning other elements of the story, there is general agreement as to the character and significance of Billy Budd and John Claggart. Billy Budd is the Handsome Sailor uniting "strength and beauty," whose moral nature is not "out of keeping with the physical make." Claggart is Billy's reverse. He is pale and unhealthy looking; his visage seems to hint of something defective or abnormal in the constitution and blood. This contrasts with the conjunction in Billy of beauty and goodness. Claggart had an "evil nature, not engendered by vicious training or corrupting books or licentious living, but born with him and innate, in short 'a depravity according to nature.'"

Melville is explicit about his desire to have Billy and Claggart taken as types of good and bad, and this, I think, is the chief argument against those who, like [F.O.] Matthiessen and [F. Barron] Freeman, consider homosexualism an aspect of the problem. For if Melville had desired to hint at homosexualism, he would not have denied its possibility; when speaking of Claggart's peculiar nature, he says, "In short the depravity here meant partakes nothing of the sordid or sensual." And speaking of Billy, he says he was "preeminently the Handsome Sailor" who, as Melville has told us in the opening pages of the book, typifies strength united to beauty. In those descriptions of Billy emphasizing his delicate color and the fine detail of his features, the point is to impress us with his purity, his aristocratic heritage, not his femininity. Melville takes care to remind the reader that Billy had thrashed the bully, Red Whiskers.

IMPLIED CRITICISM OF VERE

But it is around the third figure, Captain Vere, that the greatest disagreement has arisen. This suggests that a detailed examination of his character and function is essential to any understanding of the novel. He is described as apparently the best type of British naval man:

> always acquitting himself as an officer mindful of the welfare of his men, but never tolerating an infraction of discipline; thoroughly versed in the science of his profession, and intrepid to the verge of temerity, though never injudiciously so.

He loves to read, particularly those books "treating of actual men and events no matter of what era—history, biography and unconventional writers, who, free from cant and convention, like Montaigne, honestly, and in the spirit of common sense philosophize upon realities." In the reading he found

> confirmation of his own more reserved thoughts—confirmation which he had vainly sought in social converse, so that as touching most fundamental topics, there had got to be established in him some positive convictions which he forefelt would abide in him essentially unmodified so long as his intelligent part remained unimpaired.

This particular sentence creates a question as to Melville's meaning. Does he suggest here that the only result of Vere's reading is that his mind becomes more and more firmly fixed on his earliest opinions, that no author can ever modify them, either because he will not let their ideas penetrate or because he never reads books that do not agree with him; or does Melville imply that Vere's opinions are instinctively right and that all the books in Vere's library, "compact, but of the best" agree with him unfailingly? But it is as yet too early to decide. Melville continues to describe Vere as one whose "settled convictions were as a dyke against those invading waters of novel opinion social political and otherwise" and as one who opposed these novel opinions because they seemed to him not only "incapable of embodiment in lasting institutions, but at war with the peace of the world and the true welfare of mankind." This last phrase sounds suspiciously like cant, like sarcasm. Vere's reasons here are such terribly stock arguments that it is hard to accept them at face value.

The possibility arises that the reader is expected to understand that Vere's reasoning is presented without comment because it is simply and transparently a rationalization of an uninformed and bigoted man who reads only those authors who reinforce his views. But if this possibility is to be accepted as fact, the reader must find other implied criticism of Vere, and, indeed, it does not take much searching. Melville, for example, goes to the trouble of devoting several pages to Nelson, the greatest of English captains, pointing out with approval that Nelson challenged death by his brilliant apparel.

> Personal prudence even when dictated by quite other than selfish consideration is surely no special virtue in a military man; while an excessive love of glory, impassioning a less burning impulse the honest sense of duty, is the first.

Nelson, of course, dies a soldier's death, while Vere dies drugged and ashore before ever reaching fame. Nelson is a fighter in direct contact with the enemy; but Vere, in the encounter described in *Billy Budd*, does not have an opportunity to catch the opposing ship. Vere is frequently used for diplomatic missions, the very opposite of a captain's usual job; Vere, says Melville, though a man of "sturdy qualities was without brilliant ones." Nelson is asked to take command of a ship recently involved in the Great Mutiny, for "it was thought that an officer like Nelson was the one, *not indeed to terrorize the crew into base subjection,* but to win them, by force of his mere presence back to an allegiance if not as enthusiastic as his own, yet as true" (italics mine). Vere, in a similar situation, hangs Billy, "thinking perhaps that under existing circumstances in the navy the consequence of violating discipline should be made to speak for itself.". . .

VERE'S ARGUMENT TO THE COURT

The core of Vere's argument is that we must bow to necessity; "For that law and the rigor of it, we are not responsible. Our vowed responsibility is in this: That however pitilessly

that law may operate, we nevertheless adhere to it and administer it.'" A logical extension of this argument is that man
should abdicate responsibility for unjust law and enforce it
mechanically. Man should not try to change that which is
wrong, but merely accept injustice and tyranny and lie
supinely beneath them; man is to stand by and watch the innocent as indiscriminately ground under the heel of unre-
sisted law as are the evil.

Melville makes his opposition to this view clear by dedi-
cating the book to Jack Chase, his companion years before on
the frigate *United States.* It was this voyage that became the
story of *White-Jacket,* the novel that cried out so eloquently
against impressment, flogging, the captain's tyranny. Jack
Chase is here mentioned by name and is referred to as "a
stickler for the Rights of Man and the liberties of the world."
It would be ironic indeed to dedicate *Billy Budd* to such a
man if the novel was devoted to submission. However, the
preface helps to make clear the direction of the book. In it,
Melville speaks of the French Revolution as an expression of
"the Spirit of that Age [which] involved the rectification of the
Old World's hereditary wrongs." He points out that, although
the revolution had in its turn become an oppressor, the outcome was "a political advance along nearly the whole line for
Europeans," and he concludes by saying,

> in a way analogous to the operation of the Revolution at large
> the Great Mutiny, though by Englishmen naturally deemed
> monstrous at the time, doubtless gave the first latent prompt-
> ing to most important reforms in the British Navy.

In short, tyranny can be successfully resisted.

We can now be sure of the direction of the theme of *Billy
Budd.* In local context it suggests that it is wrong to submit
to unjust law. Those in power, such as Vere, should do all
they can to resist the evil inherent in any institution or government. All men are flawed, but not all men are depraved;
and we must not let those institutions designed to control the
evil destroy the good. In a larger context, man should not re-
sign himself to the presence of evil but must always strive
against it. It is possible to check the validity of this view by
making sure that the various incidents, descriptions, and
points reinforce it, and that they also contradict the "testament of acceptance" theory.

Observe that Vere dies drugged and on shore before he
has "attained to the fullness of fame." In other words, Vere's

end is suitable to one who did not deserve such renown as the daring and imprudent Nelson, a man capable, as Vere is not, of inspiring his men to loyalty, of substituting persuasion for coercion.

Observe that Claggart is characterized as civilized and intellectual;

> the man's even temper and discreet bearing would seem to intimate a mind peculiarly subject to the law of reason, not the less in his heart he would seem to riot in complete exemption from that law having apparently little to do with reason further than to employ it as an ambidexter implement for effecting the irrational.

But such men, continues Melville,

> are true madmen, and of the most dangerous sort, for their lunacy is not continuous but occasional evoked by some special object; it is probably secretive which is as much to say it is self contained, so that when moreover, most active it is to the average mind not distinguishable from sanity. . . .

This material comes into sharper focus when considered in relationship to Vere. He, like Claggart, is civilized; he, like Claggart, is intellectual; and he, like Claggart, uses reason to a bad end. Melville had suggested that Claggart was mad, and yet in Chapter 21, the surgeon, after seeing Claggart's body and hearing Vere say that the boy must hang, cannot banish this treasonable thought: "Was Captain Vere suddenly affected in his mind . . . ? Was he unhinged?" The surgeon reports, as instructed by Vere, to the lieutenants and the captain of the marines. "They fully stared at him in surprise and concern. Like him they seemed to think that such a matter should be reported to the Admiral." Melville pushes further; in the next chapter he says,

> Who in the rainbow can draw the line where the violet tint ends and the orange tint begins? . . . So with sanity and insanity. . . . Whether Captain Vere, as the Surgeon professionally and primarily surmised, was really the sudden victim of any degree of aberration, one must determine for himself by such light as this narrative can afford. . . .

MELVILLE'S MESSAGE: RESIST EVIL

Melville was a fighter, he was stubborn, he never accepted the easy way out. Would it not then be contradictory for him, after a lifetime of resisting practical evil in the world at large and metaphysical evil in his novels, at the very end to discover that he had been wrong all along and that his duty had always been to lie down and accept evil as unavoidable?

It is now possible to review the story swiftly. It begins with a cue from a narrator; a rebellion, like the French Revolution or the Spithead Mutiny, may result in good, although in the beginning it may not seem so. Thus, rebellion is justified in the first pages, the implication being that evil can and perhaps should be resisted. We have seen how the various characteristics of the three main actors are clues to the working out of this theme. Claggart is evil through and through; he possesses the perverted intelligence of a serpent, an intelligence used for irrational purposes. Billy Budd, on the contrary, is pure innocence, acting and judging on instinct alone. When Vere is introduced, his central characteristic is his intellection, by means of which he can justify or rationalize an over-prudence that leads to injustice. The chapter on Nelson reminds us that Vere's kind of caution and Vere's way of preventing possible mutiny are not admirable.

It may be argued that, while both Vere and Claggart possess intelligence, Vere uses his wisely and justly. But this argument collapses when it is perceived that Vere does not do what reason would suggest in so dubious a case, i.e., jail Billy until they reach land. The real point is, of course, that Vere does not act on reason and intelligence at all, but on fear; his intelligence, instead of being a guide, is a perverted instrument. Such scenes as the confusion of the officers and the doubt of the surgeon concerning Vere's sanity make sense only when regarded as putting into issue Vere's stature and ability.

It may also be argued that such episodes are intended to demonstrate that Vere and only Vere has the intelligence and insight to perceive the deeper issues. But this explanation falls to the ground when it is realized that Vere's whole argument is irrational and that his final appeal is to brute force. The ballad at the end becomes particularly rich in this context. Billy is to be sacrificed, but unjustly and unnecessarily so. The ballad, written by one of his comrades who does not understand the issues but who feels obscurely the truth of the matter in spite of a calumnious official report, speaks of Billy as unafraid but sad. Billy, being innocence personified, does not fear death; but as an unjust sacrifice, he is pictured as alone and unhappy. He longs for companionship and affection and thinks wistfully of his friends; in the end he contemplates with a melancholy resignation his death:

Fathoms down, fathoms down, how I'll dream fast asleep.
I feel it stealing now. Sentry, are you there?
Just ease these darbies at the wrist,
And roll me over fair.
I am asleep, and the oozy weeds about me twist.

Thus, Billy's cry, "God Bless Captain Vere," is the crowning irony and really the climax of the story, for he was hanged unjustly. Melville says here that a harsh truth of this harsh world is that good folk can be misled, that they can be abused by the evil simply because they are trusting. Thus Melville reminds us that we must keep up the good fight: evil must not remain uncontested. And he does so not by a call to arms but by demonstrating the consequences of unresisting acquiescence.

Ironic Social Commentary in *Billy Budd*

Karl E. Zink

In this selection, scholar Karl E. Zink concentrates on the responses of the crew to Billy's hanging. Zink considers the work ironic social commentary because the crew, from whom one would expect rebellion and revulsion, become increasingly passive, docile, and inarticulate in their responses to authority on the ship. According to Zink, Melville is pointing out the dehumanizing tyranny of "the Forms"—the impersonal, artificial rules governing society in nineteenth-century America—and he is criticizing the moral passivity which makes the mass of men complicitous in this shameful and unjust state of society.

Zink's scholarship ranges from an analysis of eighteenth-century English satiric essays, *Literary Criticism in* The Tatler, to book-length explorations of form in the work of modern American writer William Faulkner: *William Faulkner: Studies in Form and Idea* and *Flux and the Frozen Moment: The Imagery of Stasis in Faulkner's Prose.*

Billy Budd, Foretopman is a social allegory, the last of Herman Melville's criticisms of social injustice as he saw it in nineteenth century America. His critical observations began mildly and idealistically in *Typee* (1846) with his (for that time) daring denunciation of the Christian missionary in the South Pacific; and they were explicit and dramatic in *White Jacket* (1850) when Melville first symbolized the man-of-war society and damned, for example, the practice of flogging in the United States Navy. His censure of mid-century commercial American society in *The Confidence Man* (1857) was just as explicit, but a new element of irony gave this book a sophistication and power which transcended the raw rhetoric of *White Jacket.* The same basic strain of philosophical irony motivated *Billy Budd* thirty years later. In this last book he resorts to heavier symbolism and irony to dramatize his last charge against the artificial "forms" by which he saw men live blindly and passively. *Billy Budd* is a tragedy of society; not a tragedy of "hope and triumph in death," as Mr. [F. Barron] Freeman asserts in summarizing his critique of the novel, nor of "passive acceptance," or "necessity," as some thirty years of American criticism have uniformly reiterated.

Despite its apparent historical authenticity, *Billy Budd* is not a realistic novel of events. It is rather heavy social allegory. The characters and situations operate clearly as symbols. Against the social frame of the ship—the man-of-war society—it develops anew the old struggle between the force for good and the force for evil, with a special ugly twist brought into being (Melville feels) by the inherent evil of the social machinery. Billy and John Claggart are the complex symbols for these forces. Claggart is aggressive evil; Billy is passive good, a comprehensive symbol of the sort of natural goodness that Adam lived before his fall, in large part only the ignorance of evil. He is possibly an agent of Divine justice. Evil in the world has the edge; it enjoys a strong survival factor, not because of greater power but because it is nurtured and protected by the "forms" (potentially evil) by which the culture governs itself. A third symbolic character is Captain Vere, the enlightened mediator, symbol of Authority, who phrases and ponders the philosophical problem involved in Billy's fatal clash with Claggart, but who defends the harshness of the social code as ultimately best for the common good. It is Vere, as much as Billy, who dramatizes the awful power and blind impersonality of the forms. For although he, a *good* man, sensitive and intelligent, is fully aware (where Billy is not) of the injustice of the trial and the execution, he is too enmeshed in the forms himself not to enforce them. His dilemma is, of course, acute—he is many days away from the jurisdiction of the fleet admiral; the recency of the great mutinies is still an ever present threat to all naval authorities. The letter of the law simplifies; it softens the sting to the conscience of disturbing moral considerations. He too dies, soon after Billy, trammelled in his own fashion among the forms. And though Billy's name is on his lips when he dies he apparently does not regret his decision.

A fourth character, apparently overlooked for many years,

is the crew of the *Indomitable,* the mass of mankind, dominated easily, often brutally, by an authority they have
learned to fear and respect. The symbolic behavior of the
crew in response to the hanging has been long overlooked.
Prior to Billy's hanging the crew do not act as a group; they
enjoy no dynamic identity. But the execution of Billy galva-
nizes them into action and identity. They respond immediately as a mass, integrated by instinctive resistance to injustice. We shall see that in this instinctive, but pathetically
abortive, reaction of the crew to the hanging Melville asserts
his final judgment of nineteenth century America's danger-
ously immoral inclination. . . .

THE CREW'S THWARTED RESPONSE TO AUTHORITY

Every development which follows the hanging is an ironic
comment on that event and underscores the final triumph of
the forms. . . .

This crucial sequence of events begins, in fact, just before
the hanging, when Vere summons all hands during the second dog-watch to pronounce sentence. The men betray an
immediate, instinctive reaction against his announcement of
Billy's fate. But their impulse is quickly overpowered by Authority:

> Their Captain's announcement was listened to by the throng
> of standing sailors in a dumbness like that of a seated con-
> gregation of believers in hell listening to the clergyman's an-
> nouncement of his Calvinistic text.

> At the close, however, a confused murmur went up. It began
> to wax. All but instantly, then, at a sign, it was pierced and
> suppressed by shrill whistles of the Boatswain and his mates
> piping down one watch.

We must note the beginning here of characteristic terms for
the description, on the one hand, of Authority, and, on the
other, of the unorganized mass: the *dumbness,* the *confused
murmur* of the men *is pierced and suppressed* by *shrill whistles, piping.*

Later, only seconds after the awful moment of the execution, with Billy still warm and quiet against the yard, Melville is at pains to describe a second sullen murmur from the
men; this too is firmly and efficiently silenced by Authority:

> The silence at the moment of execution and for a moment or
> two continuing thereafter, a silence but emphasized by the
> regular wash of the sea against the hull or the flutter of a sail

caused by the helmsman's eyes being tempted astray, this emphasized silence was gradually disturbed by a sound not easily to be here verbally rendered. Whoever has heard the freshet-wave of a torrent suddenly swelled by pouring showers in the tropical mountains, showers not shared by the plain; whoever has heard the first muffled murmur of its sloping advance through precipitous woods, may form some conception of the sound now heard. The seeming remoteness of its source was because of its murmurous indistinctness since it came from close by, even from the men massed on the ship's open deck. Being inarticulate, it was dubious in significance further that it seemed to indicate some capricious revulsion of thought or feeling such as mobs ashore are liable to in the present instance possibly implying a sullen revocation on the men's part of their involuntary echoing of Billy's benediction. But ere the murmur had time to wax into clamor it was met by a strategic command, the more telling that it came with abrupt unexpectedness.

"Pipe down the starboard watch, Boatswain, and see that they go."

Shrill as the shriek of the sea-hawk the whistles of the Boatswain and his Mates pierced that ominous low sound, dissipating it; and yielding to the mechanism of discipline the throng was thinned by one half. For the remainder most of them were set to temporary employments connected with trimming the yards and so forth, business readily to be got up to serve occasion by any officer-of-the-deck.

Again, the instinctive feelings of the group are quelled. Note they are described as *indistinct, inarticulate, murmurous;* it is *the mechanism of discipline* which thins the throng.

When Billy's shotted hammock is dropped over the side a few moments later (all hands called again, this time to witness burial), a third strange human murmur is heard, blended this time with another "inarticulate" sound—that of the great sea-fowl hovering hungrily over the spot, "circling it low down with the moving shadow of their outstretched wings and the cracked requiem of their cries." This motion was seen by the superstitious sailors as "big with no prosaic significance"—nature too rebelled—and immediately

An uncertain movement began among them, in which some encroachment was made. It was tolerated but for a moment. For suddenly the drum beat to quarters, which familiar sound happening at least twice a day, had upon the present occasion some signal peremptoriness in it. True martial discipline long continued superinduces in an average man a sort of impulse of docility whose operation at the official sound of command much resembles in its promptitude the effect of an instinct.

This time it is the drum beat that dissipates the angry mood of the massed men. The movement is characteristically *uncertain,* but Authority as usual is brisk and sure. For the third time Melville has driven home his belief in the natural though inarticulate revulsion which the mass of men feel against the tyranny of the forms, and for the third time we have seen their vague "murmur" expertly quelled. He is most specific at this point that the average man has developed an impulse of docility in the face of Authority that is practically instinctive.

Captain Vere immediately justifies the drum beat to quarters (it is an hour earlier this Sunday morning) as necessary to counteract the temporary mood of his men:

> "With mankind" he would say "forms, measured forms are everything; and that is the import couched in the story of Orpheus with his lyre spellbinding the wild denizens of the woods."

This is the climactic, ironic cap to their *inarticulate* feelings of outrage—this easy, learned explanation, heightened by the classical allusion which betrays the great age of the entrenched power of the forms. For "Orpheus" read *Vere;* for "lyre" read *Boatswain's pipe, drum;* "spellbinding" and "wild denizens" have overtones which are immediately apparent. In the following paragraph the Chaplain conducts the customary morning service, the drum beats the retreat, and "toned by music and religious rites subserving the discipline and purpose of war, the men in their wonted orderly manner dispersed to the places allotted them when not at the guns." Note the terms *wonted, orderly, allotted.* The forms have won out. . . .

FINAL CHAPTERS CRITICIZE "THE FORMS"

To the novel Melville added three short chapters and the ballad, "Billy in the Darbies." These final chapters trace Billy's story forward in time and amplify Melville's final criticism of the forms. The first of these records the death of Captain Vere in the act of destroying the *Athéiste.* The second records the further triumph of the impersonal forms in the ironic reversal of character and fact which was preserved in the authorized weekly naval chronicle called *News from the Mediterranean*—"all that hitherto has stood in human record," Melville says with characteristic irony, "to attest what manner of men respectively were John Claggart and Billy Budd."

For here, it will be remembered, John Claggart was "vindictively stabbed to the heart by the suddenly drawn sheath knife of Budd," whom he accused of "some sort of plot . . . among an inferior section of the ship's company." Because he used a knife, Billy is presumed no Englishman but an "assassin" of foreign origin serving in the English Navy. The "enormity" of his crime and the "extreme depravity of the criminal" are deplored. The exemplary character of Claggart is there said to refute Dr. Johnson's "peevish saying" that patriotism is the last refuge of a scoundrel. "The promptitude of the punishment has proved salutary. Nothing amiss is now apprehended aboard the *H.M.S. Indomitable.*" Authority speaks. Through the high impersonality and indifference of the forms to the individual lives they dominate Billy dies unjustly and his character in the annals of men is unjustly and carelessly defamed.

The last chapter briefly traces the history of the yard from which Billy hung, how chips of it came to be cherished as pieces of the Cross, and records the composition of the ballad and how it was in time printed at Portsmouth. But this perspective, too, only reiterates man's subservience to the forms, his docility. This is manifest in the uncritical, paradoxical feeling of the men regarding the rightness of the execution:

> Ignorant though they were of the secret facts of the tragedy, and not thinking but that the penalty was somehow unavoidably inflicted from the naval point of view, for all that they instinctively felt that Billy was a sort of man as incapable of mutiny as of willful murder.

Though they cherished splinters from his spar and in their hearts felt him incapable of murder and mutiny, somehow his execution must have been justified "from the naval point of view." The murmur grows weaker.

There remains the folk record, the ballad, "Billy in the Darbies," which brings Melville's story of Billy Budd to a close. Composed by a watchmate of Billy's (a man who should have known him well), it is said to preserve "the general estimate of his nature and its unconscious simplicity." But in no satisfactory sense does it do this. This folk record tells us as little about the Billy Budd the reader knows as did the organ of the forms, *News from the Mediterranean.*

It preserves the last reflections of the condemned man on the night before he was hanged (a longer speech than Billy made anywhere in the novel), not his narrative, as might be expected, or any suggestion of his symbolic or spiritual meaning. Rough as it is, there is about it a sophistication, a bizarre humor, grim puns, that no one who knew him well could have attributed to him. Preoccupation with the ugly details of death by halter and sea burial do not bespeak the undisturbed boy who slept like a baby before his hanging. It is even doubtful that Billy ever gave an eardrop to Bristol Molly. The ballad is too passive, for one thing, and too non-committal. If the facts of his story—and his spiritual significance, as well—are thus blurred in the folk mind as well as in the official record, then mankind's immersion in the forms is blind and dark indeed. Something is missing in a ballad which generations of sailors are supposed to have sung in memory of a hero. What is missing, I suggest, is the outraged murmur which sought articulation first when sentence was pronounced, again when Billy ascended to the yard, and again when he was dropped into the sea. No spark of that "instinctive," "inarticulate," "uncertain" but genuine outrage which the massed crew had intuitively felt and abortively expressed aboard ship appears even by implication in the folk record—where it belongs. We should expect their murmur at his death to survive. But it does not. Only blurred, sympathetic feelings survive. Inasmuch as the ballad is no more valuable a record of the real Billy and no more sensitive to the spiritual Billy than it is, Melville's implication, his irony, seems clear. The men were incapable of understanding—incapable of realizing just how rare, and how innocent, and how important Billy was to the ship and to themselves. We know that Authority withheld the central facts. The several mass reactions we see the crew make are all non-rational, intuitive. (The crew's echo of Billy's benediction of Vere is irrational, coming as it does between clear manifestations of revolt.) Because their response to the injustice of the hanging was intuitive and inarticulate, it could be controlled. Melville stresses this. Apparently the men were no more capable of a vital, resistant articulation in words, than they were in action. And thus Authority perpetuates itself. This is the last of the chain of ironies following the hanging which illuminate the brute, insidious power of the forms—the great danger to the individual resident in the machinery by which the group manages itself.

A CRITICISM OF "THE FORMS" AND MEN'S MORAL PASSIVITY

We have seen resistance to the forms grow weaker with each remove from the deck of the *Indomitable*. Vere dies convinced that his decision was justified—his last words, "Billy Budd," were not the "accents of remorse." The only official documentary record of Billy's story was hopelessly distorted. His mates, cherishing splinters from his spar, knowing in their hearts he was incapable of murder and mutiny, docilely accepted the penalty as "unavoidably inflicted from the naval point of view." And, finally, the ballad, the folk record, is also a distortion, which betrays subtly the undiscriminating docility of the pliable crew. This is Melville's final irony. The murmur has been lost. The triumph of the forms is complete. And Melville's tragic allegory of nineteenth century American society is finished.

That Billy Budd had to die is to the eternal shame of the inflexible machinery that could shove him off. For it was "the forms" that nurtured and protected the evil Claggart, and an apologist for the forms (Vere) who, fully awake to Billy's moral innocence, condemned the man to die who had rid the world (symbolically) of natural evil. Mr. [Joseph] Schiffman reminds us of the terrible dramatic irony of Billy's benediction of Captain Vere. And there is deep irony in the repetition of Billy's words—"God bless Captain Vere"—by the "wedged mass of upturned faces," the docile crew, inured to passive acceptance of the rules, to worship, almost of their administrators. "God bless Captain Vere" is the last thing they would knowingly have uttered. But with Billy alone in their hearts and in their eyes, their emotional identification with him is so complete that momentarily they too reflect his own special innocence of their true dilemma. The lesson is not that Billy learns to accept the necessary harshness of the forms, but that in their high impersonality there is a dangerous lack of discrimination—dangerous to the individual and to the social structure itself. For in justifying Billy's death, the structure deprived itself symbolically of the force for good. And part of the lesson is that men tolerate this inherent evil of the structure passively, uncritically. Moral integrity is often, unhappily, endangered by or sacrificed to the impersonal dicta of the forms. Civilization has come to compromise men's cherished natural integrity and constitutes a threat to itself. Something like this, it seems to me, is the tenor of Melville's thought in *Billy Budd*. It is ironic social criticism, not acceptance.

Billy Budd Follows the Form of Classical Tragedy

Richard Harter Fogle

Richard Harter Fogle, author of *Melville's Shorter Tales* and numerous scholarly books on both English and American romantic writers, was professor of English at Tulane University when he wrote the following selection. In it, Fogle explains that *Billy Budd* resembles classical tragedy in that it presents a tragic dilemma in which one good is sacrificed to preserve another; it achieves tragic reconciliation because the sacrifice offers meaning and hope to the witnesses, Fogle explains. Fogle focuses on Captain Vere's tragic error and on the tragic irony apparent in Vere's actions. He concludes by commenting on the tragic vision Melville offers: Good earned through suffering and sacrifice is ultimately redemptive.

Richard Harter Fogle's books include *Hawthorne's Fiction, Hawthorne's Imagery, The Idea of Coleridge's Criticism, The Imagery of Keats and Shelley, The Romantic Movement in American Writing,* and *The Permanent Pleasure: Essays on Classics of Romanticism.*

Billy Budd is a tragedy, in that it presents an action of great magnitude which develops a dilemma insoluble without loss of one good in the preservation or achievement of another. Or, in other words, two different and irreconcilable systems, in this instance the order of nature and the order of the British Navy, clash directly. Captain Vere is forced to choose the order of the Navy and therefore sacrifice the innocent Billy Budd, the natural man. We sympathize with Vere, but such is the complexity of the considerations involved that we are not quite sure that he has chosen rightly; there are some grounds for arguing that the sacrifice of Billy was avoidable.

Excerpted from "*Billy Budd:* The Order of the Fall," by Richard Harter Fogle, *Nineteenth-Century Fiction*, 1960–1961. Copyright © 1960 by the Regents of the University of California. Reprinted with permission.

There is a tragic reconciliation, however, for the memory of Billy lives on as a Christ of the sailors, as a bright spot of meaning and hope against a dark background. His kingdom is not of this world, but it exists. *Billy Budd* is tragedy, too, in providing the increase of knowledge that we have rightly come to attach to tragedy. The confrontation of opposing characters in crucial action, if properly conducted, enlarges our knowledge of the potentialities of human nature and of the circumstances under which human beings exist. . . .

CAPTAIN VERE

Captain the Honorable Edward Fairfax Vere is a bachelor of forty at the time of the action of *Billy Budd*. Melville uses a dialectic method of balanced oppositions to describe him: he is of noble birth, but his advancement has not been altogether owing to his family connections; a stern disciplinarian, he is also mindful of the welfare of his men; he is "intrepid to the verge of temerity, though never injudiciously so"; a thorough seaman and naval officer, he never uses nautical terms in ordinary conversation, and is notably unobtrusive as commander of his ship. In politics he is an enlightened conservative. He represents a golden mean.

He has salient traits and qualities, however, which characterize him more sharply as an unusual man. Though practical enough when occasion demands it, he "would at times betray a certain dreaminess of mood." He is exceptionally bookish, and he reads deeply, in "confirmation of his own more reserved thoughts," and to establish settled principles by study of the past. His fellow officers find him a little pedantic; he cannot quite accommodate his thought and conversation to the "bluff company" of men "whose reading was mainly confined to the journals." Thus he has not quite the tact of a man of the world; he is too honest and direct to pay careful heed to immediate circumstances. His nickname, "Starry" Vere, has come upon him accidentally from a kinsman who had been reading [seventeenth-century English poet Andrew] Marvell's "Appleton House," with the lines

This 'tis to have been from the first
In a domestic heaven nursed
Under the discipline severe
Of Fairfax and the starry Vere.

The connection is casually made, but the association of "discipline severe" with the captain is nevertheless worth pointing out. A lover of order, he is devoted to duty and discipline, and certainly to self-discipline. . . .

VERE'S TRAGIC ERROR

So much for Vere's character. To proceed to his actions, their wisdom and their honesty are open to question, but this must always be true of any man's conduct when faced with a tragic dilemma. We sense that the Captain must play his predestined part in the tragic drama. If he is guilty of a tragic error, it is in his insistence upon secrecy throughout, or perhaps more largely in his acceptance of all responsibility for decisions. Yet here again, the tragic circumstance is unusual, the natures of the men he deals with exceptional, and chance by accumulation takes on the purpose and the power of fate.

To rehearse the situation of *Billy Budd,* it is of course abnormal because of the recent mutinies at Spithead and the Nore. The year 1797 is a time of crisis for the British Navy; there is no leisure for extended reflection. Then, it happens that Vere is unusually isolated. Because of a lack of frigates in the English squadron the *Indomitable,* though a line-of-battle ship, is on detached scouting duty, partly because of her exceptional sailing qualities and partly because of Vere's reputation for reliability and initiative. The circumstances conspire to produce tragedy. Vere is approached by his master-at-arms, with whom it happens by chance that he is not well acquainted, with a tale of treason in a common sailor, Billy Budd. Behind the charge lies a monstrous tangle of malice and misunderstanding, of which Vere can know nothing. Nevertheless he judges correctly that Claggart's accusation is false. Among the difficulties and ambiguities of the situation is the fact that the skillful and subtle Claggart is strangely clumsy. He overplays his hand; one would say that he is fey, struck by some unconscious premonition of approaching death, or maddened by irrational hatred. This oddity, however, rather confuses than clarifies.

Convinced of Claggart's falseness, Vere arranges a private confrontation, but with the object rather of testing the accuser than of trying the accused. By hindsight we can see that this decision of Vere's is fatal, since the private interview ends with the death of Claggart, struck down by a single blow of the man he has slandered, too unexpected and sudden for prevention. Yet in the circumstances Vere's choice of action would seem eminently judicious.

TRAGIC IRONY

Again, Vere contributes to the fatal result indirectly by his very insight and his kindliness, as in his insight into Claggart. He correctly interprets Billy's agonized dumbness before the accusation, but his kindness has precisely the opposite effect from his intentions.

> Though at the time Captain Vere was quite ignorant of Billy's liability to vocal impediment, he now immediately divined it, since vividly Billy's aspect recalled to him that of a bright young schoolmate of his whom he had seen struck by much the same startling impotence in the act of eagerly rising in the class to be foremost in response to a testing question put to it by the master. Going close up to the young sailor, and laying a soothing hand on his shoulder, he said: "There is no hurry, my boy. Take your time, take your time." Contrary to the effect intended, these words so fatherly in tone, doubtless touching Billy's heart to the quick, prompted yet more violent efforts at utterance—efforts soon ending for the time in confirming the paralysis, and bringing to the face an expression which was as a crucifixion to behold. The next instant, quick as the flame from a discharged cannon at night, his right arm shot out, and Claggart dropped to the deck.

Vere immediately foresees the full consequences, as his first word indicates. "'Fated boy,' breathed Captain Vere in tone so low as to be almost a whisper, 'what have you done!'" Henceforth he is to be the agent of the Fates, or perhaps the banishing angel of the latter Fall.

The Captain's behavior in the following moments is suspicious, almost mad, to the eye of an observer. The ship's surgeon is immediately summoned. A prudent, poised, and experienced man, he is an excellent witness. His shock, however, comes from his limited understanding of what he witnesses. Vere's conduct is perfectly intelligible by the light of his own superior insight.

> Suddenly, catching the Surgeon's arm convulsively, he exclaimed pointing down to the body—"it is the divine judgment of Ananias! Look! . . ." Captain Vere was now again motionless standing absorbed in thought. But again starting, he vehemently exclaimed—"Struck dead by an angel of God. Yet the angel must hang!"

The surgeon is further disturbed by Vere's disposition of the body in a compartment of his cabin, as implying an unaccountable desire for secrecy; and, as we have seen, in this respect Vere is consistently laid open to suspicion. The possibility that he is wrong, or even that he is evil, is steadily before us. Yet a reasonable reading demonstrates that Vere's estimate of the situation, affected as it is by mutiny and war, is correct. A fallen and corrupted world can only be governed by the stern provisions of the Mutiny Act, carried out with the utmost speed and decision. No time can be permitted for doubt or speculation by those who might mutiny; in his secrecy Vere is defending an indispensable order. The surgeon is a calm and experienced man of the world, but Vere is more than a man of the world. He is as it were a seer and priest, endowed with intuitive knowledge of the human heart and spirit, well-fitted, and alone well-fitted on the battleship *Indomitable*, to comprehend two such extraordinary human beings as Claggart and Billy Budd. Along with them he belongs to a different order of nature from common humanity. . . .

MELVILLE'S TRAGIC VISION

At the court-martial Vere is at first slow to speak, but his hesitation comes of considering how best to fit his words to the capacities of his hearers. "Similar impatience as to talking is perhaps one reason that deters some minds from addressing any popular assemblies."

> When speak he did, something both in the substance of what he said and his manner of saying it, showed the influence of unshared studies modifying and tempering the practical training of an active career. This, along with his phraseology now and then was suggestive of the grounds whereon rested that imputation of a certain pedantry socially alleged against him by certain naval men of wholly practical cast. . . .

Vere thus represents something of Melville's own isolation in age and society, and symbolized in the circumstances of the writing itself of *Billy Budd*, a work for long unpublished. This isolation does not at all preclude an anxious solicitude for the times, and a desire to set men right. Vere may be said to be preaching the necessity of tragedy to his good-natured and reluctant officers, and so, on the whole, is Melville. In a complacent and optimistic age he asserts the doctrine "now popularly ignored," of the Fall of Man, and directs attention to the neglected words of Holy Writ, to which he recurs.

> And, indeed, if that lexicon which is based on Holy Writ were any longer popular, one might with less difficulty define and denominate certain phenomenal men. As it is, one must turn to some authority not liable to the charge of being tinctured with Biblical element. . . . Dark sayings are these, some will say. But why? Is it because they somewhat savor of Holy Writ

in its phrase mysteries of iniquity? If they do, such savor was foreign from my intention for little will it commend these pages to many a reader of today.

The irony is minatory [menacing, threatening]. Vere also uses the phrase, "a mystery of iniquity," in lecturing to his officers.

Neither Melville nor Vere is denying the possibility of progress and the existence of Providence. The rejection of materialist optimism does not preclude the hope that all may yet be well. More than once in *Billy Budd* it is said that the French Revolution, once deemed an unmixed evil, has functioned in a design to bring about an ultimate good, in which the sacrifice of Billy has its mysterious place as well. But Melville and Vere maintain that this good can come about only through suffering and tragic action; there are no short cuts, no easy solutions. The Original Sin has alienated man from nature, and therefore no natural code can fitly govern human society. War is a sin; the mutiny at the Nore is a sin against order; and their consequences are the Articles of War and the Mutiny Act. Yet the alienation is not total, we are not wholly estranged from the natural and the divine; and sacrifice can redeem. . . .

A REDEMPTIVE SACRIFICE

Until the sacrifice is consummated the Original Sin is in power. Its consequences cannot be evaded. "Their Captain's announcement was listened to by the throng of standing sailors in a dumbness like that of a seated congregation of believers in hell listening to the clergyman's announcement of his Calvinistic text." Extraordinary measures are taken, therefore, to ensure that the ceremony is fitly carried out. Special precautions are taken that none shall communicate with Billy (save the Chaplain, whose services as Christian priest are irrelevant at this grim observance and unneeded by the victim himself). Certain parts of the ceremony are imperceptibly altered or hastened as the immediate circumstances dictate; regularity is consistently preserved by slight irregularities. Thus at a threatening murmur of the crew its entity as a congregation is suddenly destroyed by calling the starboard watch. "Shrill as the shriek of the sea-hawk the whistles of the Boatswain and his Mates pierced that ominous low sound, dissipating it; and yielding to the mechanism of discipline the throng was thinned by one half." The comparison suggests the cruel bird of prey, perhaps the exultant emissary of a fierce sky-god, like the hawk that was dragged to destruction with the sinking *Pequod* in *Moby Dick.* This, with its implications, is an aspect of the meaning that cannot be ignored, but at the same time it is only one aspect of a very complex totality. To return to the progress of events, Billy's body is then buried with all expedition, "with a promptitude not perceptibly merging into hurry, though bordering that." But "a second strange human murmur was heard" when sea birds pass close to the ship and hover over the spot where the body has vanished into the sea. . . .

[T]he birds that come to the burial of Billy Budd have a dual significance. They are supernatural, but do they mourn or exult? Are they the emissaries of a god of nature who is outraged and pitiful, or of an authoritarian sky-god, like [nineteenth-century poet Percy Bysshe] Shelley's Jupiter, who forever oppresses the natural man, the "people" of the *Indomitable* and of the world? For Melville's purposes they are both, though these meanings are contradictory; since the possibilities of the situation itself are ambiguous and contradictory.

Immediately upon the second murmur of the crew the drum beats to quarters. "At this unwonted muster at quarters, all proceeded as at the regular hour." The religious ceremony in which Billy Budd had been sacrificed to the observance of the Mutiny Act concludes formally, in terms specifically liturgical.

> The band on the quarter-deck played a sacred air. After which the Chaplain went through with the customary morning service. That done, the drum beat the retreat, and toned by music and religious rites subserving the discipline and purpose of war, the men in their wonted orderly manner dispersed to the places allotted them when not at the guns.

There is plainly a sharp irony in this mingling of Christianity and war. Vere is the real priest, the Chaplain only a simulacrum. Yet the tragedy must be played out, the redemption must be bought by the blood of the Lamb, and Vere and Billy must take their allotted parts.

Ambiguity in *Billy Budd*

Barbara Johnson

Attentiveness to the text makes it clear that Melville
designed a novel with "ragged edges," scholar Barbara Johnson contends. In this selection, Johnson
examines how Melville makes both the plot and the
characters ambiguous rather than asserting an authoritative position. The characters' actions are the
reverse of what one would expect: the innocent Billy
kills, the evil Claggart dies a victim, and the wise
Vere hangs a blameless man. The characters themselves defy easy definition. Billy is not just simply
good, Johnson points out; he is a "naïve reader,"
who accepts appearances and censors the negative
to maintain his naïve perspective. Claggart, the
enigma who prompts others to propagate rumors to
explain his character, is an ironic doubter; he dis-
trusts appearances and suspects evil behind every
flower, but he never doubts anyone who confirms
his own suspicions. Melville's revisions of Vere's
character make him particularly difficult to judge. In
Johnson's view, Melville has created a text with
gaps, "deadly spaces," which prevent readers from
making easy definitive judgements of the work.

A well-known critical theorist, Barbara Johnson's most
recent work includes *Consequences of Theory*, co-edited
with Jonathan Arac, *Freedom and Interpretation*, and *The
Feminist Difference: Literature, Psychoanalysis, Race, and
Gender*.

The plot of Melville's *Billy Budd* is well known, and, like its
title character, appears entirely straightforward and simple.
It is a tale of three men in a boat: the innocent, ignorant foretopman, handsome Billy Budd; the devious, urbane master-
at-arms, John Claggart; and the respectable, bookish commanding officer, Captain the Honorable Edward Fairfax

Excerpted from "Melville's Fist: The Execution of *Billy Budd*," by Barbara Johnson,
Studies in Romanticism, Winter 1979. Copyright © 1979 by the Trustees of Boston University. Reprinted with permssion.

("Starry") Vere. Falsely accused by Claggart of plotting mutiny aboard the British man-of-war *Bellipotent,* Billy Budd, his speech impeded by a stutter, strikes his accuser dead in front of the Captain, and is condemned, after a summary trial, to hang.

In spite of the apparent straightforwardness of the facts of the case, however, there exists in the critical literature on *Billy Budd* a notable range of disagreement over the ultimate meaning of the tale. . . .

THE THREE CENTRAL CHARACTERS

As Charles Weir puts it, "The purely physical action of the story is clear enough, and about its significant details there is never any doubt. . . . It is, therefore, with some consideration of the characters of the three principal actors that any analysis must begin." "Structurally," writes F.B. Freeman, "the three characters *are* the novel."

Melville goes to great lengths to describe both the physical and the moral characteristics of his protagonists. Billy Budd, a twenty-one-year-old "novice in the complexities of factitious life," is remarkable for his "significant personal beauty," his "reposeful good nature," his "straightforward simplicity," and his "unconventional rectitude." But Billy's intelligence ("such as it was," says Melville) is as primitive as his virtues are pristine. He is illiterate, he cannot understand ambiguity, and he stutters.

Claggart, on the other hand, is presented as the very image of urbane, intellectualized, articulate evil. Although "of no ill figure upon the whole," something in Claggart's pallid face consistently inspires uneasiness and mistrust. He is a man, writes Melville, "in whom was the mania of an evil nature not engendered by vicious training or corrupting books or licentious living, but born with him and innate, in short, 'a depravity according to nature.'" The mere sight of Billy Budd's rosy beauty and rollicking innocence does not fail to provoke in such a character "an antipathy spontaneous and profound."

The third man in the drama, the one who has inspired the greatest critical dissent, is presented in less vivid but curiously more contradictory terms. The *Bellipotent*'s captain is described as both unaffected and pedantic, dreamy and resolute, irascible and undemonstrative, "mindful of the welfare of his men, but never tolerating an infraction of discipline," "intrepid to the verge of temerity, though never injudiciously so." While Billy and Claggart are said to owe their characters to "nature," Captain Vere is shaped mainly by his fondness for books:

> He loved books, never going to sea without a newly replenished library, compact but of the best. . . . With nothing of that literary taste which less heeds the thing conveyed than the vehicle, his bias was toward those books to which every serious mind of superior order occupying any active post of authority in the world naturally inclines: books treating of actual men and events no matter of what era—history, biography, and unconventional writers like Montaigne, who, free from cant and convention, honestly and in the spirit of common sense philosophize upon realities.

Vere, then, is an honest, serious reader, seemingly well suited for the role of judge and witness that in the course of the story he will come to play.

No consideration of the nature of character in *Billy Budd*, however, can fail to take into account the fact that the fate of each of the characters is the direct reverse of what one is led to expect from his "nature." Billy is sweet, innocent, and harmless, yet he kills. Claggart is evil, perverted, and mendacious, yet he dies a victim. Vere is sagacious and responsible, yet he allows a man whom he feels to be blameless to hang. It is this discrepancy between character and action that gives rise to the critical disagreement over the story. . . .

DISCREPANCIES BETWEEN CHARACTER AND ACTION

The fact that Melville's plot requires that the good act out the evil designs of the bad while the bad suffer the unwarranted fate of the good indicates that the real opposition with which Melville is preoccupied here is less the static opposition between evil and good than the dynamic opposition between a man's "nature" and his acts, or, in [William York] Tyndall's terms, the relation between human "being" and human "doing."

Curiously enough, it is precisely this question of "being" versus "doing" that is brought up by the only sentence we ever see Claggart directly address to Billy Budd. When Billy accidentally spills his soup across the path of the master-at-arms, Claggart playfully replies, "Handsomely done, my lad! And handsome *is* as handsome *did* it, too!" (emphasis mine). The proverbial expression "handsome *is* as handsome *does*," from which this exclamation springs, posits the possibility of a continuous, predictable, transparent relationship between

"being" and "doing." It supposes that the inner goodness of
Billy Budd is in harmonious accord with his fair appearance, that, as Melville writes of the stereotypical "Handsome
Sailor" in the opening pages of the story, "the moral nature"
is not "out of keeping with the physical make." But it is precisely this continuity between the physical and the moral,
between appearance and action, or between "being" and
"doing," that Claggart questions in Billy Budd. He warns
Captain Vere not to be taken in by Billy's physical beauty:
"You have but noted his fair cheek. A mantrap may be under
the ruddy-tipped daisies." Claggart indeed soon finds his
suspicions confirmed with a vengeance: when he repeats
his accusation in front of Billy, he is struck down dead. . . .

BILLY IS NOT SIMPLY GOOD

As many critics have remarked, Billy's character seems to
result mainly from his exclusion of the negative. When informed that he is being arbitrarily impressed for service on
a man-of-war, Billy "makes no demur." When invited to a
clandestine meeting by a mysterious stranger, Billy acqui-
esces through his "incapacity of plumply saying *no*." But it is
interesting to note that although Billy thus seems to be "just
a boy who can't say no," almost all the words used to describe him are negative in form: in-nocent, un-conventional,
il-literate, un-sophisticated, un-adulterate, etc. And although
he denies any discrepancy between what is said and what is
meant, he does not prove to be totally incapable of lying.
When asked about the shady visit of the afterguardsman, he
distorts his account in order to edit out anything that indicates any incompatibility with the absolute maintenance of
authority. He neglects to report the questionable proposition
even though "it was his duty as a loyal blue jacket" to do so.
In thus shrinking from "the dirty work of a telltale," Billy
maintains his "plotlessness" not spontaneously but through
a complex act of filtering. Far from being simply and naturally pure, he is obsessed with maintaining his own irre-
proachability in the eyes of authority. After witnessing a
flogging, he is so horrified that he resolves "that never
through remissness would he make himself liable to such a
visitation or do or omit aught that might merit even verbal
reproof." Billy does not simply exclude the negative: he re-
presses it. His reaction to questionable behavior of any sort
(Red Whiskers, the afterguardsman, Claggart) is to obliter-

ate it. He retains his *"blank* ignorance" only by a vigorous act of erasing. As Melville says of Billy's reaction to Claggart's petty provocations, "the ineffectual speculations into which he was led were so disturbingly alien to him that *he did his best to smother them"* (emphasis mine).

> In his *disgustful recoil* from an overture which, though he but ill comprehended, he *instinctively knew* must involve evil of some sort, Billy Budd was like a young horse fresh from the pasture suddenly inhaling a vile whiff from some chemical factory, and by repeated snortings trying to *get it out* of his nostrils and lungs. This frame of mind *barred all desire* of holding further parley with the fellow, even were it but for the purpose of gaining some enlightenment as to his design in approaching him. (emphasis mine)

Billy maintains his purity only through constant, though unconscious, censorship. "Innocence," writes Melville, "was his blinder.". . .

CLAGGART IS AN ENIGMA

John Claggart is presented as an enigma for cognition, a man "who for reasons of his own was keeping *incog"* (emphasis mine). Repeatedly referred to as a "mystery," Claggart, it seems, is difficult, even perilous, to describe:

> For the adequate comprehending of Claggart by a normal nature these hints are insufficient. To pass from a normal nature to him one must cross "the deadly space between." And this is best done by indirection.

Between Claggart and a "normal nature," there exists a gaping cognitive chasm. In a literal sense, this image of crossing a "deadly space" in order to reach Claggart can be seen almost as an ironic prefiguration of the murder. Billy does indeed "cross" the "space" between himself and Claggart by means of a "deadly" blow. The phrase "space between" recurs, in fact, just after the murder, to refer to the physical separation between the dead Claggart and the condemned Billy:

> Aft, and on either side, was a small stateroom, the one now temporarily a jail and the other a dead-house, and a yet smaller compartment, leaving a *space between* expanding forward. (emphasis mine)

It is by means of a deadly chiasmus [rhetorical term indicating a "criss-cross" arrangement: "Pleasure's a sin, and sometimes sin's a pleasure"] that the spatial chasm is crossed.

But physical separation is obviously not the only kind of "deadly space" involved here. The expression "deadly space between" refers primarily to a gap in cognition, a boundary beyond which ordinary understanding does not normally go. This sort of space, which stands as a limit to comprehension, seems to be an inherent feature of the attempt to describe John Claggart. From the very beginning, Melville admits: "His portrait I essay, but shall never hit it.". . .

Melville takes up the question of Claggart's "nature" many times. Each time, the description is proffered as a necessary key to the understanding of the story. And yet, each time, what we learn about the master-at-arms is that we cannot learn anything:

> Nothing was known of his former life.

> About as much was really known to the *Bellipotent*'s tars of the master-at-arms' career before entering the service as an astronomer knows about a comet's travels prior to its first observable appearance in the sky.

> What can more partake of the mysterious than an antipathy spontaneous and profound . . . ?

> Dark sayings are these, some will say. But why? Is it because they somewhat savor of Holy Writ in its phrase "mystery of iniquity"? . . .

The lack of knowledge of Claggart's past, for example, is seen as a sign that he has something to hide:

> Nothing was known of his former life. . . . Among certain grizzled sea gossips of the gun decks and forecastle went a rumor perdue that the master-at-arms was a *chevalier* [Melville's italics] who had volunteered into the King's navy by way of compounding for some mysterious swindle whereof he had been arraigned at the King's Bench. *The fact that nobody could substantiate this report was, of course, nothing against its secret currency.* . . . Indeed a man of Claggart's accomplishments, without prior nautical experience entering the navy at mature life, as he did, and necessarily allotted at the start to the lowest grade in it; a man too who never made allusion to his previous life ashore; these were circumstances which *in the dearth of exact knowledge* as to his true antecedents opened to the invidious *a vague field for unfavorable surmise.*

In other words, it is precisely the absence of knowledge that here leads to the propagation of tales. The fact that nothing is known of Claggart's origins is not a simple, contingent, theoretically remediable lack of information: it is the very *origin* of his "evil nature." Interestingly, in Billy's case, an equal lack of knowledge leads some readers to see his origin as divine. Asked who his father is, Billy replies, "God knows.". . .

BILLY'S WAY OF READING VS. CLAGGART'S

It seems evident that Billy's reading method consists in taking everything at face value, while Claggart's consists in seeing a mantrap under every daisy. Yet in practice, neither of these methods is rigorously upheld. The naive reader is not naive enough to forget to edit out information too troubling to report. The instability of the space between sign and referent, normally denied by the naive reader, is called upon as an *instrument* whenever that same instability threatens to disturb the *content* of meaning itself. Billy takes every sign as transparently readable as long as what he reads is consistent with transparent peace, order, and authority. When this is not so, his reading clouds accordingly. And Claggart, for whom every sign can be read as its opposite, neglects to doubt the transparency of any sign that tends to confirm his own doubts: "the master-at-arms *never suspected the veracity*" of Squeak's reports. The naive believer thus refuses to believe any evidence that subverts the transparency of his beliefs, while the ironic doubter forgets to suspect the reliability of anything confirming his own suspicions.

Naiveté and irony thus stand as symmetrical opposites blinded by their very incapacity to see anything but symmetry. Claggart, in his antipathy, "can really form no conception of an *unreciprocated* malice." And Billy, conscious of his own blamelessness, can see nothing but pleasantness in Claggart's pleasant words: "Had the foretopman been conscious of having done or said anything to provoke the ill-will of the official, it would have been different with him, and his sight might have been purged if not sharpened. As it was, innocence was his blinder." Each character sees the other only through the mirror of his own reflection. Claggart, looking at Billy, mistakes his own twisted face for the face of an enemy, while Billy, recognizing in Claggart the negativity he smothers in himself, strikes out.

The naive and the ironic readers are thus equally destructive, both of themselves and of each other. It is significant that both Billy and Claggart should die. . . .

VERE'S METHOD OF READING

While Billy and Claggart read spontaneously and directly, Vere's reading often makes use of precedent (historical facts, childhood memories), allusions (to the Bible, to various ancient and modern authors), and analogies (Billy is like Adam, Claggart is like Ananias). Just as both Billy and Claggart have no known past, they read without memory; just as their lives end with their reading, they read without foresight. Vere, on the other hand, interrogates both past and future for interpretative guidance.

While Budd and Claggart thus oppose each other directly, without regard for circumstance or consequence, Vere reads solely in function of the attending historical situation: the Nore and Spithead mutinies have created an atmosphere "critical to naval authority," and, since an engagement with the enemy fleet is possible at any moment, the *Bellipotent* cannot afford internal unrest.

The fundamental factor that underlies the opposition between the metaphysical Budd/Claggart conflict on the one hand and the reading of Captain Vere on the other can be summed up in a single word: history. . . .

MELVILLE MAKES VERE AMBIGUOUS

The opposing critical judgments of Vere's decision to hang Billy are divided, in the final analysis, according to the place they attribute to history in the process of justification. For the ironists, Vere is misusing history for his own self-preservation or for the preservation of a world safe for aristocracy. For those who accept Vere's verdict as tragic but necessary, it is Melville who has stacked the historical cards in Vere's favor. In both cases, the conception of history as an interpretive instrument remains the same: it is its *use* that is being judged. And the very fact that Billy Budd criticism itself historically moves from acceptance to irony is no doubt itself interpretable in the same historical terms.

Evidence can in fact be found in the text for both pro-Vere and anti-Vere judgments:

> Full of disquietude and misgiving, the surgeon left the cabin. Was Captain Vere suddenly affected in his mind?

> Whether Captain Vere, as the surgeon professionally and privately surmised, was really the sudden victim of any degree of aberration, every one must determine for himself by such light as this narrative may afford.

> That the unhappy event which has been narrated could not have happened at a worse juncture was but too true. For it was close on the heel of the suppressed insurrections, an aftertime very critical to naval authority, demanding from

every English sea commander two qualities not readily inter-
fusable—prudence and rigor.

Small wonder then that the *Bellipotent*'s captain . . . felt that
circumspection not less than promptitude was necessary. . . .
Here he may or may not have erred.

The effect of these explicit oscillations of judgment within the
text is to underline the *importance* of the act of judging while
rendering its outcome undecidable. Judgment, however difficult, is clearly the central preoccupation of Melville's text,
whether it be the judgment pronounced by Vere or upon him.

There is still another reason for the uncertainty over
Vere's final status, however: the unfinished state of the manuscript at Melville's death. According to editors Hayford and
Sealts, it is the "late pencil revisions" that cast the greatest
doubt upon Vere; Melville was evidently still fine-tuning the
text's attitude toward its third reader when he died. The ultimate irony in the tale is thus that our final judgment of the
very reader who takes history into consideration is made
problematic precisely by the intervention of history: by the
historical accident of the author's death. History here affects
interpretation not only within the content of the narration
but also within the very production of the narrative. And
what remains suspended by this historical accident is nothing less than the exact signifying value of history itself.
Clearly, the meaning of "history" as a feature distinguishing
Vere's reading from those of Claggart and Budd can in no
way be taken for granted.

The Work Is a Testament to Melville's Own Spirit

Robert Milder

In this article Professor Robert Milder suggests that
Billy Budd is a testament to Melville's own hard-
earned sense of self-worth. Two collections of verse
which Melville published privately while working on
Billy Budd, John Marr and Other Sailors (1888) and
Timoleon (1891), reveal Melville's personal quarrel
with society and God, and his doubt of the value of
his commitment to art. These themes are also seen in
Billy Budd, Milder explains. Milder thinks that Melville began the novel as a fable illustrating the fate of
innocence in an evil world, then developed it into an
indictment of God who is responsible for man's
temptation, fall, and, because of His subsequent neglect of man, the continuation of evil in the world.
Two articles on the *Somers* incident, in which three
sailors were hanged for conspiracy, may have moved
Melville to develop the character of Vere and shift the
emphasis of the work to a tragedy of governance,
Milder speculates. Significantly, Melville's concern
with the injustice of this world, the remoteness of
God, and the tragedy of governance recedes in Melville's final revisions. According to Milder, the focus
shifts to two tragically doomed individuals, Billy and
Vere, who with compassion and understanding, face
tragedy. Milder sees in the final revisions Melville's
own earned recognition of self-worth in spite of the
world's neglect of his work and the impossibility of
knowing for sure if suffering is salvific.

In addition to editing *Critical Essays on Melville's Billy
Budd, Sailor*, Robert Milder has published an edition of the
novel and several short works, *Billy Budd and Selected*

Excerpted from "Melville's Late Poetry and *Billy Budd:* From Nostalgia to Transcendence," by Robert Milder, *Critical Essays on Melville's* Billy Budd, Sailor, (Boston: G.K.
Hall & Co., 1989). Copyright © 1989 by G.K. Hall & Co. Reprinted with permission.

120

Tales. He has also co-edited, with John Bryant, *Melville's Evermoving Dawn: Centennial Essays.*

Ever since it first appeared in Raymond Weaver's edition of 1924, *Billy Budd* has impressed readers as a testament of one kind or another, most commonly of Christian acceptance or of irony and political protest. More properly, *Billy Budd* is the product not of a single unified fictive intention but of successive intentions that span the course of Melville's retirement and link the narrative to [his verse collections] *John Marr* and *Timoleon.* Begun in or around 1886 as a sailor monologue akin to those in *John Marr, Billy Budd* evolved through three major stages, together with several important substages, and was chronologically complete and awaiting final revision when Melville died in 1891. . . . The text we now read, constructed from a genetic analysis of the manuscript, is as close to Melville's final intention as scholars can make it. Even so, *Billy Budd* remains a thematically sequential work whose shifts of interest replicate its compositional history and reflect Melville's inward journey over the last five years of his life.

Though the compositional evidence surrounding *Billy Budd* has been available since 1962, interpreters have rarely drawn upon it to read *Billy Budd* as a work in process. Yet the shape of Melville's 1888 narrative is largely inferable, and by using its themes as a point of reference it is possible to trace the pattern of Melville's late career and at the same time suggest the unfolding logic that governs the final text. In brief, *John Marr* and *Timoleon* show Melville still quarreling with Providence and society, uncertain of the value of his long dedication to art, and divided between a bleak awareness of human tragedy and a fond retrospection. Originating in the nostalgia and despair of *John Marr, Billy Budd* developed by 1888 into a last arraignment of God and society—a design that shaped the work, with changing emphasis, until Melville surmounted his anger during the final stages of composition and arrived at the only "testament" he could make, or would ever have wanted to make, a testament to his own spirit.

NOSTALGIA AND DESPAIR IN *JOHN MARR*

Privately printed in an edition of twenty-five copies, *John Marr* sounds the notes that will dominate Melville's final period: solitude and alienation; a yearning for the color and heroism of wooden ship days; and a gray, unflinching acceptance of life's mischances as they occur against the backdrop of nature's blankness. In the title poem with its long prose headnote, Melville dramatized his isolation through the figure of an aging ex-sailor living miles inland and drawn in his loneliness to memories of his former shipmates. The thematic center of the poem is a contrast between two human communities fronting nature: "staid" landsmen toiling on the oceanic prairie, their social "unresponsiveness . . . of a piece with the apathy of Nature herself," and sailors from a glorified past "Hoisting up the storm-sail cheerly, / *Life is storm— let storm!*" A vision of free-spirited camaraderie amid nature's hardships also informs "Jack Roy," Melville's eulogy to Jack Chase, his messmate from the *United States* and the *beau idéal* of *White-Jacket* (1850) whom Melville would honor again in the dedication to *Billy Budd.* The key virtue in both poems is "geniality," defined in the prologue to "John Marr" as "the flower of life springing from some sense of joy in it, more or less.". . .

SELF-QUESTIONING IN *TIMOLEON*

Less deliberately organized than *John Marr, Timoleon* is most distinguished for those poems that explore the renunciations and rewards of truth's votaries—the female astronomer in "After the Pleasure Party"; the recluse of "The Garden of Metrodorus"; the artists of "The Weaver," "In a Garret," and "Art"; the insomniac thinker of "The Bench of Boors"; and the light-seeker of "The Enthusiast"—as if Melville, surveying his long career, were trying to persuade himself he had not been a Fool of Truth. As in *John Marr,* the title poem governs the collection. Adapted from Plutarch's story of the Corinthian soldier and statesman (with hints from Balzac's *The Two Brothers*), *Timoleon* is a compendium of Melville themes and a loose allegory of his emotional life: a docile second son overshadowed by his active brother, "the mother's pride and pet"; the son heroically committing himself to virtue (Timoleon slaying his tyrant-brother Timophanes; Melville pursuing truth in his fiction regardless of sales or reputation); and the son, repudiated by his mother and estranged from a weak-hearted populace, exiling himself from the city and railing at the silent gods for their abandonment of "earnest natures." In plot and rhetoric *Tim-*

oleon recalls *Pierre* [1852] when, having sacrificed worldly happiness for truth, Pierre finds himself despised by earth and heaven, mother and divine Father, alike. Yet where Pierre dies scorning the gods, society, and the noblest part of himself, Melville ends "Timoleon" with a vision of triumph in which the hero emerges from retirement to save the state, then—"Absolved and more!"—spurns Corinth's praise and returns to voluntary exile.

The question that frames "Timoleon" is whether glory, belatedly won, is the result of "high Providence, or Chance," a question much on Melville's mind as he pondered his long neglect, too proud or vulnerable to respond to the modest overtures of the New York literati yet scarcely indifferent to posthumous fame. . . .

BILLY BUDD: CRITICIZING THE WAYS OF GOD AND MAN

Written contemporaneously with *John Marr* and *Timoleon* and drawing its themes partly from the same urgencies, *Billy Budd,* during its long evolution, can be understood as a working through of Melville's bitterness toward a remote Providence and a small-souled, neglectful world.

In its opening eulogy of the 'Handsome Sailor' who flourished in "the less prosaic time" before steamships, *Billy Budd* recalls the nostalgia of "John Marr" and "Jack Roy." What had been sentimentality in the verse, however, is immediately raised to myth as the pre-lapsarian Billy is impressed from the *Rights-of-Man* and introduced to "the ampler and more knowing world of a great warship," Melville's symbol, as in *White-Jacket,* for the great world itself. Melville's first intention in opposing Claggart and Billy was probably to illustrate the fate of good-natured innocence amid the mantraps of society, a theme since *Typee* (1846) but one that "John Marr" had focused on the class of sailors—"Barbarians of man's simpler nature, / Unworldly servers of the world." As Melville reworked his manuscript, however, Claggart's motiveless spite became a "'mystery of iniquity'" that savored of "Holy Writ," and *Billy Budd* developed from an exemplary fable to a reenactment of the Christian fall that raised the problem of an omnipotent God's responsibility for evil.

Melville's literary paradigm at this stage of composition was *Paradise Lost,* and echoes of [John] Milton's Satan resound in the expanded portrait of Claggart. Yet lacking the climactic execution scene that some readers interpret as

Melville's Christian acceptance, the 1888 *Billy Budd* seems
rather an anti–*Paradise Lost* designed to impugn the ways of
God. The early narrative concluded with the garbled report
of events from "News from the Mediterranean," upon which
Melville moralized: "Here ends a story not unwarranted by
what sometimes happens in this [one undeciphered word]
world of ours—Innocence and infamy, spiritual depravity
and fair repute." "Sometimes happens" implies a periodic
divine negligence of the sort Ishmael [in *Moby-Dick*] called
"all interregnum in Providence," and it establishes the injustice done Billy as a recurrent historical fact, comple-
menting the mythic status of the action as a representation
of the fall. God is thus arraigned on two counts: his ultimate
responsibility for man's temptation and fall—Claggart acts
out his part "like the scorpion for which the Creator alone is
responsible"—and his general *ir*responsibility toward hu-

THE *SOMERS* INCIDENT

*Herman Melville's cousin, Guert Gansevoort, was first lieu-
tenant of the American warship USS* Somers *during its
maiden voyage in 1842. The crew of 120 consisted mainly of
boys under the age of twenty who were in training for the
American Naval Service. Off the coast of Africa Gansevoort was
told of a planned mutiny. On December 1, 1842, three men were
hanged aboard the* Somers *for alleged mutiny.*

In November 1842 the *Somers,* cruising off Africa, was affected
by what we would regard today as a seizure of collective hys-
teria. Lt Gansevoort was informed that there was a mutiny
planned, and he immediately told Commander Alexander
Slidell Mackenzie (1803–48). The ringleader of the mutiny was
alleged to be Midshipman Philip Spencer, nineteen years old,
and the son of John C. Spencer (1788–1855), Secretary of War
in [President John] Tyler's cabinet. Spencer and two others
were arrested. An informal court of inquiry was conducted by
First Lieutenant Guert Gansevoort and the other officers, but
they reported to the Commander that the evidence did not appear conclusive. The only concrete evidence was a list drawn
up by Spencer in Greek, dividing the crew into probables, pos-
sibles, and those who would be allowed to survive because
they possessed special skills. It may all have been a prank;
there had been no overtly mutinous act. But Commander
Mackenzie told the officers through Lt Gansevoort

that it was evident these young men [the junior officers] had man affairs ever since. Also arraigned are those official versions of events (naval chronicles, Christian apologetics) that play havoc with the truth in order to demonstrate that all goes well. An "inside narrative," in his context, would be one that set the metaphysical record straight and, incidentally, adjusted the wrongs of worldly reputation. . . .

A TRAGEDY OF GOVERNANCE

It may have been the act of recording his protest that freed Melville from its emotional grip, as had happened years earlier with *Moby-Dick;* yet catharsis alone cannot explain the new direction his narrative took. Two magazine articles on the *Somers* incident of 1842, the first appearing in the spring of 1888 as Melville worked on *John Marr,* may have kindled Melville's memories of his cousin Guert Gansevoort, a first lieutenant on the *Somers* when an acting midshipman and

---

wholly misapprehended the nature of the evidence . . . and that there would be no security for the lives of officers or protection to commerce if an example was not made in a case so flagrant as this. It was my duty, he urged, to impress these views upon the court. I returned and did, by impressing these considerations, obtain a reluctant conviction of the accused.

Midshipman Spencer and two others were hanged at the yardarm on December 1. The *Somers* returned to New York on the 14th, and the 'mutiny' soon became a *cause célèbre.* Those elements in American society which saw in authority, hierarchy and social discipline a necessary corrective to the abuses of democracy came to the defence of Mackenzie. The 'judicial murder' of Spencer became the rallying cry for democrats; in their eyes the actions of Mackenzie and the response of the Navy was an example of the Federalist and Whig traditions perverting the course of justice for their own interests. . . .

To avoid a civilian trial, Slidell Mackenzie requested a court martial and was duly acquitted in April 1843. Fenimore Cooper had initially accepted the account of the mutiny which Slidell Mackenzie gave at the Court of Inquiry, but he became restless with the manner of the defence, which he described as 'a medley of folly, conceit, illegality, feebleness and fanaticism'. Partisans on both sides were pleased to find their views widely shared.

Eric Homberger, "Melville, Lt. Guert Gansevoort and Authority: An Essay in Biography." In *New Perspectives on Melville,* edited by Faith Pullin. Kent, OH: The Kent State University Press, 1978.

two sailors were hanged for conspiracy, and prompted Melville to brood on questions of justice and authority. Whatever the reason, Melville returned to his manuscript and addressed the thinly drawn figure of Vere, a shift of focus that carried the action forward beyond Claggart's death without requiring Melville substantially to recast what he had written. Claggart with his violet eyes and Billy with his welkin-blue had been less—or more—than roundly human characters, but with Claggart's death the fall and its attendant interests became a given and the story descended to the naturalistic world of gray-eyed Vere (comfortably or not, Melville's intellectual home) in which moral and political questions had to be resolved in post-lapsarian terms against "the monotonous blank of the twilight sea."

It was the tragedy of governance—a new subject for him—that absorbed Melville now and drew him outward beyond his frustrations, first toward the political world, then toward the psyche, with a humaneness and breadth of comprehension unapproached in the late poetry. In Part 4 of *Clarel* Melville had voiced the negatives of his social thought through the ex-Confederate officer Ungar, on one side a blooded Indian who rails at injustice with the rage of the dispossessed, on the other a lapsed-Catholic reactionary who berates radicals and flabby progressives for their neglect of original sin. *Billy Budd* preserves the terms of Ungar's neither/nor in its harsh portrayal of French Jacobinism and British repression, but it focuses upon the empowered ruler who must act. The long trial scene in Chapter 21 is a masterpiece of ambiguity, with Vere in one reading an anguished but duty-bound representative of the political state, in another a myopic conservative whose narrow and exacting application of a wartime code tyrannical in itself is a double indictment of a martial society that sacrifices justice to order and dehumanizes even its most conscientious men. That both readings are not merely justified but demanded by the text is a sign that Melville requires of us something more than ideological choice or a painless, "literary" tolerance of alternatives. Convinced of the need for social bulwarks against nature's chaos—Vere's "forms, measured forms"—Melville knew that any particular forms were likely to be radically flawed. He knew, also, that forms had to be administered by human beings enmeshed in events and compromised by their tendencies, limitations, passions, and interests. We are all familiar with the duck/rabbit figure that seems to defy a simultaneous perception of rival shapes. In *Billy Budd* Melville presents a circumstanced "case" with more perspectives on it—and attitudes toward it—than a mortal consciousness can comfortably entertain, and he challenges us to rise to it as a representation of tragic experience in its irreducible and overwhelming truth. . . .

TRAGICALLY DOOMED INDIVIDUALS

After an initial movement upward from exemplary fable to theological myth, *Billy Budd*, during its long gestation, traveled progressively downward toward the particularized world of human action. Novelists commonly speak of their characters escaping the roles assigned them and generating unforeseen action as if from themselves. The shifts in Melville's novels had always had a different source—the logic of his inward discoveries—but in *Billy Budd* Melville seems genuinely to be responding to the latent possibilities of his story and, at the end, to the forward pull of Vere and Billy themselves. Where the late poetry had lent itself to an allegorized brooding on social and metaphysical injuries, the action of *Billy Budd* gradually lifted Melville out of himself and turned him from the objectification of private trials to an absorbed concern with how tragically doomed individuals might behave.

One looks to an authorial explanation of this kind because nothing in Melville's characterization and themes adequately prepares us for the ending of this narrative. Vere's speech to the drumhead court shows human beings hopelessly entangled in the real or mind-forged manacles of their condition. Yet Billy's trial concluded, the focus of the narrative shifts again as issues of justice and political morality give way to the purely human circumstance of two men meeting the inevitable with generosity and strength. The Vere who had argued for coolness during the trial scene is "melt[ed] back into what remains primeval in our formalized humanity" and softened by the weight of a judgment made conscientiously and with full awareness of tragic sacrifice, disastrously wrong as it may be. Billy's role—to feel Vere's pain more than his own—is greater still, but his growth is made visible only at the last when, "spiritualized now through late experiences so poignantly profound," he becomes, not a symbol of Christ, but an example of humanity's Christlike capacity for self-transfiguration. Billy's "fortunate fall," reminiscent of Donatello's in [Nathaniel Hawthorne's] *The Marble Faun* but without sin, is a justification neither of God's ways nor of the ways of the state. Billy's triumph is personal and has reference to the moral life alone. The "soft glory" that "chanced" to illuminate "the vapory fleece hanging low in the East" seems a version of the divine signet craved by Timoleon and Pierre, but its promise is indistinct and we are immediately recalled to our unsanctified world by the image of Billy swaying lifelessly in the "slow roll" of a "great ship ponderously cannoned." By this time, however, the injustices of the human world and the remoteness of the divine have ceased to matter. A mood of hushed contemplation has descended upon the narrative, and along with the witnessing sailors we marvel at the timeless heroism of human beings trapped by circumstances and swayed by the imperatives of their nature yet capable toward the last of an extraordinary gesture of magnanimity.

Like Shakespeare's late romances (as Northrop Frye describes them), *Billy Budd* encloses tragedy within a movement "from a lower world of confusion to an upper world of order" and suggests the "transformation from one kind of life to another"; it "outrag[es] reality and at the same time introduc[es] us to a world of childlike innocence which has always made more sense than reality." In *Billy Budd*, however, this upper world is solely the property of the individual, whose transformation neither regenerates the social world nor is properly understood by it. Thus Melville ends *Billy Budd* by having plodding officialdom garble Billy's story and the crewmen fashion a cult of Billy-as-Christ from a nobility it is theirs to imitate. Such will always be the world's judgments, Melville implies; yet missing from his closing ironies (so distant in tone from the bitter didacticism of the 1888 conclusion) is a concern that the travesties of reputation have any bearing on human apotheosis [deification], which knows itself by the inward sign of spiritual repleteness.

AN EARNED SENSE OF INWARD WORTH

Ultimately, the exaltation to which *Billy Budd* testifies toward the last is neither Billy's nor Vere's but the author's own. It seems especially significant that in describing Vere's communication of the verdict to Billy Melville disclaims the omniscience of narrative report and suspends his governing convention of delivering the truth. The scene is offered as a private speculation, evoked with reverence and rendered in a prose as conscious of its own quiet sublimity as of Billy's and Vere's. Though it is ostensibly the characters who claim our attention, the language of the scene, fraught with hypotheticals, continually recalls us to its origin in the sensibility of the narrator. Eloquent in its reserve, the scene hints of depths that cannot be shared with the reader, though they are plumbed with a priestly awe by the narrator himself: "But there is no telling the sacrament, seldom if in any case revealed to the gadding world, wherever under circumstances at all akin to those here attempted to be set forth two of great Nature's nobler order embrace. There is privacy at the time, inviolable to the survivor; and holy oblivion, the sequel to each diviner magnanimity, providentially covers all at least."

To the Melville of *Timoleon* "holy oblivion" would have been a fearful oxymoron signifying at once God's betrayal of human hopes for immortality and the susceptibility of all life and reputation to time. In the present context the words assume an opposite meaning: the sufficiency of time-bound greatness to itself. For Billy and Vere, the "diviner magnanimity" is to have reached a level of compassion and understanding that has not obviated tragedy but risen admirably to face it; for Melville, it is to have imagined such a possibility of behavior and have given it full allegiance. Without accommodating himself to the universe, Melville has come to accept the incongruities of what Auden calls the "human position" of suffering, and though he is unsure there can be any other position, any transcendent justification for the sufferer, he has grown to feel that the spiritual is no less divine for being located entirely within the human soul and going unrecognized by the world. In *Clarel* Melville had portrayed his idealized *alter ego,* Rolfe, as living undramatically at humanity's best without suspecting that this itself is divinity. By the closing scenes of *Billy Budd* Melville seems to have realized what Rolfe did not and to have ventured beyond both the nostalgia and despair of *John Marr* and the self-questioning of *Timoleon.* He has arrived at a certainty of inward worth and, thereby, at a qualified peace.

CHAPTER 3

Themes in *Billy Budd*

Civilization Is at War with Human Nature in *Billy Budd*

C.N. Manlove

University of Edinburgh professor C.N. Manlove explores one of *Billy Budd*'s central themes in this selection. Manlove finds the relationship between civilization and human nature to be critical in the novel. By civilization he means the state, its laws, and the military that supports it; by human nature he means the rights of the individual as well as natural sympathy and an intuitive sense of justice and truth. Manlove explains that Captain Vere articulates this conflict between civilization and human nature when he directs his officers to override human feeling in the interest of preserving the order of law during the deliberations of the court. Manlove contends that civilization is put on trial in *Billy Budd* and found to be based on self-interest and self-protection; civilization is thus aligned with the savage impulses of primitive animals which it was supposedly organized to supersede.

Manlove has written many books including *Literature and Reality, 1600–1800, The Gap in Shakespeare: The Motif of Division from* Richard II *to* The Tempest, *The Impulse of Fantasy Literature, C.S. Lewis: His Literary Achievement, Critical Thinking: A Guide to Interpreting Literary Texts, Christian Fantasy from 1200 to the Present,* and *The Chronicles of Narnia: The Patterning of a Fantastic World.*

The central theme in [*Billy Budd*] may be put as the relation of nature and civilization. The larger context of the narrative is, first, the war against revolutionary France, a revolution which, however tyrannical its eventual outcome, expressed the rebellion of human nature against despotic custom, energy against order, flux against conservative stasis; and, second, within this background, the ever-present fear of mutiny in the British navy since the rebellions at Spithead and the Nore in the same year of 1797. In this sense civilization is at war with nature in the form of the rights of man: and it is from a merchant ship of just that latter name that Melville has Billy Budd pressed aboard the warship *Bellipotent.* On the *Bellipotent,* Billy, who is presented as primally innocent, accidentally kills the evil master-at-arms Claggart when the latter provokes him in front of Vere, the captain, with a false accusation of mutinous plotting. The slaying of a superior officer is, formally, an act of mutiny: with the spectres of the Nore and Spithead before him, Vere feels he must take unhesitating action and convenes an instant drumhead court. The trial of Billy is conducted by Vere in terms of the warfare of civilization with nature: he acknowledges to his fellow-officers the claims of natural sympathy for the innocent Billy, while asserting that those claims must be overridden:

NATURAL SYMPATHY VS. CIVILIZATION'S LAWS

'But your scruples: do they move as in a dusk? Challenge them. Make them advance and declare themselves. Come now; do they import something like this: If, mindless of palliating circumstances, we are bound to regard the death of the master-at-arms as the prisoner's deed, then does that deed constitute a capital crime whereof the penalty is a mortal one. But in natural justice is nothing but the prisoner's overt act to be considered? How can we adjudge to summary and shameful death a fellow creature innocent before God, and whom we feel to be so?—Does that state it aright? You sign sad assent. Well, I too feel that, the full force of that. It is Nature. But do these buttons that we wear attest that our allegiance is to Nature? No, to the King. Though the ocean, which is inviolate Nature primeval, though this be the element where we move and have our being as sailors, yet as the King's officers lies our duty in a sphere correspondingly natural? So little is that true, that in receiving our commissions we in the most important regards ceased to be natural free agents. When war is declared are we the commissioned fighters previously consulted? We fight at command. If our judgments approve the war, that is but coincidence. So in other particulars. So now. For suppose condemnation to follow these present proceedings. Would it be so much we ourselves that would condemn as it would be martial law operating through us? For that law and the rigor of it, we are not responsible. Our vowed responsibility is in this: That however pitilessly that law may operate in any instances, we nevertheless adhere to it and administer it.

But the exceptional in the matter moves the hearts within you. Even so too is mine moved. But let not warm hearts betray heads that should be cool. Ashore in a criminal case, will an upright judge allow himself off the bench to be waylaid by some tender kinswoman of the accused seeking to touch him with her tearful plea? Well, the heart here, sometimes the feminine in man, is as that piteous woman, and hard though it be, she must here be ruled out.'

Some particular points emerge from this. One is that Vere argues that the existence of law removes moral responsibility from its agents: he partly tempts his officers with a means of smothering their consciences. Secondly, the maintenance and operation of law are shown as depending not infrequently on neglect of the basic principles of right and wrong on which they are ostensibly founded. Third, Vere is stating here a code of conduct which of itself would not be sufficient justification—and is not, to his fellow-officers—for so summary a trial and execution as he is bent on carrying out. Behind the totem of the maintenance of law lies in fact a simple fear that if Billy is not hung as an example, the omnipresent threat of mutiny may be fomented into acts aboard the *Bellipotent:* and it is this monition, as no other, that finally sways Vere's fellow-officers in the court. That is, principles are here a mask for self-preservation. Fourth, the analogy between Billy's case and that of the tearful kinswoman of the accused is inapposite, for in the latter case the prisoner may well be a guilty man in motive as well as in act: by thus dividing Billy's innocence from his act Vere perpetrates something not far removed from a lie. Lastly, we notice from the passage that Vere associates Nature with the sea: indeed just previously we have seen him pacing the cabin to and fro athwart, 'in the returning ascent to windward climbing the slant deck in the ship's lee roll, without knowing it symbolizing thus in his action a mind resolute to surmount difficulties even if against primitive instincts strong as the wind and the sea.' Elsewhere he describes revolution as a roaring flood tide. It is clear that the struggle in this story is in one way that of land with sea—the rigid, the static and the conscious with the mobile and the unconscious. In terms of Billy's fate we have the impact of a voluntaristic view of all human behaviour—if he killed Claggart, then he must be treated as having intended to—on an involuntary, instinctual mode of life.

SELF-INTEREST AND SELF-PROTECTION UNDERGIRD CIVILIZATION

Melville has made much of his story a test-case of civilization: in the pure and irresistible form of Billy Budd and his unintended deed, he sets out the rights of a man essentially innocent, opposed and destroyed by a human law which demands inhuman allegiance. Civilization is shown as ultimately a juggernaut, and the foundation of law and duty, apparently made by men for their happier society, becomes revealed as destructive of human nature, whether that which is reluctant to enforce the law, or that which suffers its rigour. Melville later extends the point to the role of the ship's chaplain aboard the *Bellipotent:*

> Marvel not that having been made acquainted with the young sailor's essential innocence the worthy man lifted not a finger to avert the doom of such a martyr to martial discipline. So to do would not only have been as idle as invoking the desert, but would also have been an audacious transgression of the bounds of his function, one as exactly prescribed to him by military law as that of the boatswain or any other naval officer. Bluntly put, a chaplain is the minister of the Prince of Peace serving in the host of the God of War—Mars. As such, he is as incongruous as a musket would be on the altar at Christmas. Why, then, is he there? Because he indirectly subserves the purpose attested by the cannon; because too he lends the sanction of the religion of the meek to that which practically is the abrogation of everything but brute Force.

Religion and morality, twin bastions of civilization, are seen in the crucible of war as stemming in the final analysis not from any absolute sense of good and evil or of justice, but from motives of self-interest and the preservation of the *status quo*. To the plea that Billy 'purposed neither mutiny nor homicide', Vere replies:

> 'Surely not. . . . And before a court less arbitrary and more merciful than a martial one, that plea would largely extenuate. At the Last Assizes it shall acquit. But how here? We proceed under the law of the Mutiny Act. In feature no child can resemble his father more than that Act resembles in spirit the thing from which it derives—War.'

The unnatural usage of the closing natural analogy could not be more pointed. War is not the exception, but the exception that must prove the rule. The trial we are given here is not only of Billy, but of civilization itself: if when tested it is found wanting, then whatever justice and charity may prevail on land in time of peace are rendered nebulous. In this analysis Melville not only prognosticates some of the special inhumanities of modern civilization, but demonstrates to his own satisfaction the primal roots of all civility in that savage impulse of self-protection and survival evident in naked form not only in the first man, but throughout the animal kingdom since the beginnings of life. In short, he postulates the view that civilization and the darker aspects of nature are not in this sense finally opposed. . . .

CIVILIZATION REJECTS BOTH TRUTH AND THE INDIVIDUAL

When all is said of Vere's character and motives, his remark before proceeding to judgment on Billy Budd must reflect ironically on himself, reducing the significance even of the better of his impulses—"'intent or non-intent is nothing to the purpose'": the repulsive act is everything; what worthy or innocent motives lie behind it, nothing. By his unveracious refusal of Budd's intentions Vere must in the last analysis forfeit consideration of his own. In this sense we must judge him by his acts alone.

Had Vere not been captain, had one of his more 'salted' officers been in his place, Billy's trial would have been deferred—with possibly happier outcome. But Melville himself insists on the exceptional natures of his characters. He makes Vere as he does because he wants as both judge and accused a man who is at once an exemplar of the best in 'landed' civilization and one actively engaged in its defence at sea. He pushes this civilization into a tight corner by having Billy's crime set within the contexts both of the lonely struggle of Britain against the forces of revolution abroad, and of the fear of mutiny at home. At the same time, however, he makes this crime one committed in total innocence, and on someone whose evil was primal and whose death was a positive good. Melville's aim is thus to sharpen the conflict to an extreme; thereby to show, first, how the survival of civilization is founded ultimately on the rejection of the individual and of truth, and second, that such rejection involves alignment with Claggart and the forces of darkness. On this latter point, the debased newspaper report of the episode, which Melville outlines at the end of his story, and in which Vere is seen as the righteous defender of order and the Claggarts of this world, has ironic truth.

Melville Probes the Mysterious Truths of the Human Heart in *Billy Budd*

James McIntosh

A key theme that links all three principal characters in *Billy Budd* is the mystery of the human heart, according to University of Michigan professor James McIntosh. None of the characters speaks all that he feels. The heart of each character is hidden from the casual observer, but it is revealed by means of body language, unguarded speech, and the narrator's use of poetic image at critical moments in the text. For instance, Melville's narrator resists describing what is actually said when Vere speaks privately to Billy after the court has met, but the narrator suggests that it is a deeply spiritual heartfelt exchange by mentioning Abraham and Isaac and by phrasing the description with considerable self-conscious hedging. The narrator's descriptions of changing facial expressions at key moments in the text are particularly instructive when attempting to discover the truth in the hearts of the characters, McIntosh claims. The narrative sequence covering Billy's execution and death engages the reader's heart and mind, McIntosh explains, by inviting appreciation of the sacred and marvelous while also insisting that readers reflect about the incident described.

James McIntosh has written books on three other nineteenth-century American writers: *Thoreau as Romantic Naturalist: His Shifting Stance Toward Nature*, *Nathaniel Hawthorne's Tales: Authoritative Text, Backgrounds, Criticism,* and *Nimble Believing: Dickinson and the Unknown.*

The mystery of the human heart is a theme that links all the principal characters in *Billy Budd*, and for Melville this mystery seems to have been one of his key preoccupations in all the stages of composition except the earliest. It is thus a key subject in the text as a whole that helps bind its disparate parts together. Though the heart cannot be explained systematically and is a sealed book to worldly reason, it may manifest itself spontaneously in moments of crisis, especially in the expression of a man's body or in his unguarded speech. Hence a sympathetic observer may note its manifestations, and conjecturally imagine the inner history of his characters.

Because the heart cannot be known by rational understanding alone, the narrator is habitually cautious in his assertions about what goes on emotionally inside the persons in his story. His syntax is typically conjectural concerning the *Bellipotent*'s sailors' feelings when they echo Billy's blessing of Captain Vere: "And yet . . . Billy alone *must have been* in their hearts, even as in their eyes" (my italics); or again concerning Vere's secret career motivations: his "spirit . . . 'spite of its philosophic austerity *may yet have* indulged in the most secret of all passions, ambition" (my italics). In Vere's case especially we cannot know what was in his heart; "ambition" may or may not explain certain features of his behavior. The reader, as often, is provoked to puzzle out the mystery in a character.

In key scenes, moreover, Melville suggests the difficulty of knowing his characters not only by hedging his observations syntactically but also by manipulating different modes of narration. Rather than simply telling his story, he makes his narrator's presence obtrusively felt, thereby confirming his own "latitude" as a writer in [Nathaniel] Hawthorne's school. A signal instance of willfully unusual narration is the scene between Billy and Vere after Billy has been condemned to death by the drumhead court. Melville demands that the reader attend to the conjectural character of his rendering of this exchange of hearts. As the narrator puts it, "what took place at this interview was never known," though "some conjectures may be ventured." After this opening the narrator engages in a virtuoso display of conjectures.

> It would have been in consonance with the spirit of Captain Vere should he on this occasion have concealed nothing from the condemned one. . . . On Billy's side it is not improbable that such a confession would have been received in much the

same spirit that prompted it. Not without a sort of joy, indeed, he might have appreciated the brave opinion of him implied in his captain's making such a confidant of him. . . . Captain Vere in end may have developed the passion sometimes latent under an exterior stoical or indifferent. He . . . may . . . have caught Billy to his heart, even as Abraham may have caught young Isaac on the brink of resolutely offering him up in obedience to the exacting behest.

The double negatives, the unassertive assertions, the stream of subjunctive constructions involving Abraham and Isaac as well as Billy and Vere—all this self-conscious hedging consorts strangely with the simple and powerful passions enacted in the scene. It is as if the narrator is engaged in thwarting the reader's wish for the direct expression of heightened affection at a climactic moment. But the point of this stylistic ingenuity and indirection is a serious one, which the narrator himself articulates later in the chapter. "There is no telling the sacrament . . . wherever . . . two of great Nature's nobler order embrace. There is privacy at the time." What Hawthorne calls "the inmost Me" remains private. The reader is admonished to remember this even with respect to characters in fiction, for in fiction too one must learn to reverence the heart's magnanimity in such persons as Billy and Vere.

BODY LANGUAGE AND POETIC IMAGE REVEAL THE HEART

Through his manipulation of this scene the narrator parades the principle, operative throughout his story, that the deepest spiritual events in the lives of his characters are hidden from an outside observer. "Holy oblivion" covers not only the most heart-felt exchanges between persons, but also the essential changes that go on in a single person. For example, the narrator can only speculate what transpires within Captain Vere while he broods over Claggart's body immediately after Billy's fatal blow:

Captain Vere with one hand covering his face stood to all appearance as impassive as the object at his feet. Was he absorbed in taking in all the bearings of the event . . . ? Slowly he uncovered his face; and the effect was as if the moon emerging from eclipse should reappear with quite another aspect than that which had gone into hiding. The father in him . . . was replaced by the military disciplinarian.

The narrator evokes Vere's impassive "appearance," and then the transformation of his "aspect," as if to infer the change in him from "the father" to "the military disciplinarian" by interpreting the seeming change in his gestures and features. Moreover, the image by means of which he imagines this change, the moon emerging from eclipse, is quintessentially mysterious. He signals with this image as well as with his questioning, conjecturing style that he guesses the truth about Vere from a distance rather than knowing it from within. In such a scene the truth of the human heart is revealed "by cunning glimpses," to adopt the language of Melville's early review of Hawthorne's *Mosses from an Old Manse.* For just because Melville insists that the heart is a mystery does not mean that one cannot dramatize it. It is a mystery with an ongoing life; and it reveals itself in dramatic and poetic images if not in definitive explanations. Thus a master of the "Art of Telling the Truth" may with luck and industry embody it in an inside narrative.

Often in *Billy Budd,* these images that evoke the heart are images of the human body. Like "The Birthmark" (or *The Scarlet Letter,* or *The House of the Seven Gables*) [by Nathaniel Hawthorne] *Billy Budd* is full of passages in which the heart speaks through the body. Billy's stutter, we recall, is provoked by "strong heart-feeling." But his active goodness of soul also appears in his bodily expression. His face is "lit . . . from within . . . The bonfire in his heart made luminous the rose-tan in his cheek." Later, when Billy lies in irons on the gundeck after the agony of his trial, the narrator observes a change in his face—"the skeleton in the cheekbone at the point of its angle was just beginning delicately to be defined under the warm-tinted skin"—and then comments, "In fervid hearts self-contained, some brief experiences devour our human tissue as secret fire in a ship's hold consumes cotton in the bale." His heart, though spiritual and unknowable, nonetheless shows itself transparently in the wasting away of his physical substance.

Claggart is hardly so transparent a character as Billy. Hypocrite that he is, he habitually conceals the lawless "riot" in his heart beneath a "discreet bearing." Yet his bodily appearance tends to betray him to those less trusting than Billy. In the soup-spilling incident, for example, he wears for the reader and for any messmates who can observe him a "bitter smile, usurping the face from the heart." When he walks away from the mess and is left to his own thoughts the smile becomes a "distorting expression," scaring a drummer-boy who collides with him by chance. The next time we see him he brings his tale of Billy the mutineer to Captain Vere, and Vere immediately suspects him. "Something . . . in [his] aspect . . . provoke[d] vaguely repellent distaste." Then when he accuses Billy before Vere his evil nature is luridly expressed through his eyes, which change color from "rich violet" to "muddy purple," and protrude "like the alien eyes of certain uncatalogued creatures of the deep. The first mesmeristic glance was one of serpent fascination; the last was as the paralyzing lurch of the torpedo fish."

With Claggart as with Billy, then, Melville relies on the body to express the heart, and portrays transformations of character through a painterly display of changing physical images. . . .

Because Vere has both a realistic sense of practical needs and a poetic intuition of human depths, he is the only character who can articulate the problem of the heart's mystery even when his attention is focused on the practical problem of how to maintain military authority. Yet his mixed nature is also tragic. He is forced to make tragic choices between the probable and ordinary course of events as he foresees them and the truth of the human heart as he intuitively perceives it. He chooses not to attend to his intimations of the mysterious insofar as they affect his performance of his duty. This choice, though it goes against the "instincts" of his own heart, is dictated by his fate as an officer of the King. "A 'mystery of iniquity,'" he says, is "a matter for psychologic theologians to discuss." The malice in Claggart's heart is, with a pun, "hardly material" when a military court must pronounce sentence on a sailor who strikes a master-at-arms. As an instrument of the court, Vere insists that "the heart . . . must here be ruled out" and that the jury must decide the case only on the basis of "the [outward] facts." For this is war and "War looks but to the frontage, the appearance."

By focusing exclusively on the public facts of the case Vere commits himself to an "outside narrative," while his choice causes terrible suffering for his inner man and, one may argue, hastens Billy's tragic death. On the other hand, another choice he makes, to come to Billy with magnanimity of heart in their closeted interview after the judgment of the court, leads to his mysterious expression of affection or peace of mind at the story's end. In another reported, conjectured scene he dies murmuring "Billy Budd, Billy Budd," not with "accents of remorse" but with a feeling no one names. Again, and at the last, the truth of his heart expresses itself in passionate words the reader catches at without benefit of explanation.

In his inside narrative, then, Melville would reveal the truth of the human heart by cunning glimpses into its mysterious tenderness or depravity. Like Hawthorne he means to burrow "into the depths of our common nature" in order to shed light on hidden passions that scarcely show themselves in conventional social intercourse. The better realism of his authentic narrative will perforce be charged with the elements of romance, so that it may be true to the depths of the heart. A merely social or worldly or scientific treatment of men such as Claggart, Billy, and Vere would miss their essence and remain superficial.

BILLY'S EXECUTION AND DEATH

A sequence toward the end of the narrative not only reenacts Melville's mockery of mere worldly knowledge with respect to the affairs of the heart, but also shows him adding a flavor of the marvelous to the dish he offers his readers. In his outwardly tactful, yet privately outlandish use of the marvelous he would seem almost to parody Hawthorne's second precept for romance in the *Seven Gables* preface. The texture of moods in the sequence is complex, modulating from the narrator's initial wonder at Billy's spiritual strength to his bemusement at the inability of commonsense men of the world to fathom him. The sequence begins in chapter 25, after Captain Vere is pictured standing "erectly rigid as a musket in the ship-armorer's rack." Then the narrator presents a contrasting image of Billy "ascending" amid "the full rose of the dawn," surrounded by clouds "shot through with a soft glory as of the fleece of the Lamb of God seen in mystical vision." The heightened language prepares the reader for the phenomenal event that follows: "In the pinioned figure arrived at the yard-end, to the wonder of all no motion was apparent, none save that created by the slow roll of the hull in moderate weather, so majestic in a great ship ponderously cannoned." When a moment later the "glorified" clouds vanish, the clear air that remains has a "serenity . . . like smooth white marble." A religious image imposed on the natural setting is thus displaced by an aesthetic one before that too disappears in the texture of ordinary narrative prose. Was the vision of Billy against the rose of the dawn a religious epiphany or a momentary theatrical illusion played out against the blankness of nature? The text vacillates serenely between belief and unbelief in the epiphany. We do not know what happens at death, which is itself a mysterious event in the life of the human heart. Yet Melville apparently wants to leave open the possibility that there may actually be a spiritual presence "out there" that welcomes Billy or that Billy "takes" as he ascends. Even if the impression of Billy's transcendence is an illusion, the poetic awe the narrator expresses may still be a genuine religious emotion, a valid expression of the human will to believe in the spirit when faced with the unknown. The text respects these religious feelings without necessarily endorsing them. Toward the mystery of Billy's death it conveys a stance of reverent agnosticism.

When Billy is hanged, "to the wonder of all" his body betrays no sign of a muscular spasm. This, of course, does not happen in ordinary experience. Normally, a hanged man jerks grotesquely; according to popular folklore at least, he also has an erection. In chapter 26 the purser and the surgeon, two quintessentially average men of the world, discuss this apparent minor miracle. The purser, the more open-minded of the two, strains with English decorousness to find language that will help him understand Billy's state of mind at such a moment; for he is anxious in a confused way to give the event a spiritual rather than a merely mechanical cause. "What testimony to the force lodged in will power," he first exclaims; and after the surgeon dismisses "will power" as an unscientific term the purser asks more meekly, "was the man's death . . . a species of euthanasia?" meaning an easy death free from pain and struggle. "Will power" and "euthanasia," however tentatively used by the purser, are words that describe Billy's inner activity or condition, either his preternatural self-restraint that calms the motions of his body at the hanging, or his utter peace of mind in death, a peace appropriate for one who has blessed his executioner.

The caustic surgeon, however, has no use for this language of the heart. He dismisses the event as unaccountable and negligible; he prefers to go about his business as if it had not happened. He corresponds to the "respectable witness" at the climax of [Hawthorne's] *The Scarlet Letter* who claims never to have seen the letter revealed on Dimmesdale's breast. Like them, he refuses to acknowledge a "ghastly miracle" that symbolizes the secret efforts of a person's will and heart, lest it affect his settled ignorance of man's inner condition. He stands for the modern skeptic in all of us who must be exorcized if we are to read a narrative that focuses on the secret inner life of its characters. In *Billy Budd*, however, his skepticism is a frivolous minority position. The common bluejackets, who represent Hawthorne's "great heart of mankind" in the story, feel instinctively that what happened at Billy's death is somehow miraculous. Their impression of his goodness and innocence is "deepened by the fact that he was gone, and in a measure *mysteriously* gone" (my italics).

In his manuscript Melville called the exchange between the purser and the surgeon "a digression" and forcibly wedged it into one of the most affecting scenes he ever wrote, placing it between Billy's hanging and the haunting responsive murmur of the crew a moment later. The effect of this interpolation, so disruptive of a "realistic" illusion, is to remove us from our involvement in the drama and force us to inquire into its meaning, particularly the meaning of "the prodigy of repose in the form suspended in air." As often in Hawthorne, we are drawn away from a "prodigy"—a marvelous event—in order to contemplate it. The purser even provides us with two partially satisfactory alternative explanations for the prodigy (will power and euthanasia), and Melville, in the style of Hawthorne, implicitly invites us to seek for others. By means of his digression Melville promotes a Hawthornean alienation effect in which the reader reflects not only on imperial politics and class divisions but also on the mysterious affections and unspoken struggles of Billy's heart. Finally, another effect of the digression is to call attention to Melville's narrative procedures, to the latitude he enjoys in manipulating his materials. By withdrawing us from the action Melville lets us know, as often in *Billy Budd*, that he exercises the special privilege of the romancer, the privilege of authorial and narrative freedom.

Polar Views of the French Revolution as a Theme in *Billy Budd*

Cyndy Hendershot

In this selection, scholar Cyndy Hendershot contends that the novel can be read within the context of two central books about the French Revolution. Edmund Burke's *Reflections on the Revolution in France* (1790) discredits the revolution as chaotic, irrational, and unnatural; Thomas Paine's *The Rights of Man* (1791–1792) takes the opposite position and argues that monarchy and the hierarchy that sustains it is irrational and unnatural. Hendershot explains that the narrator and Captain Vere in *Billy Budd* share the views of Burke, while Billy Budd, who was impressed from the merchant ship *The Rights of Man*, is viewed by them as the revolutionary threat. Significantly, the narrator and Vere, like Burke, discredit the French Revolution by describing it in negative, feminine terms; both also describe Billy and the threat he represents as feminine. According to Hendershot, the execution of Billy removes the feminized revolutionary threat of chaos and mutiny and reasserts the vision of British masculine authority.

Cyndy Hendershot has also written *The Animal Within: Masculinity and the Gothic.*

Discussions of Herman Melville's *Billy Budd, Sailor* (1891) have moved away from the "testament of acceptance"/"testament of resistance" debates about the author's view of Vere's character they were caught in for many years. The conservatism of early criticism of the novel has given way to recent studies which have contributed much-needed explorations of gender and sexuality. This article explores *Billy Budd,* bringing to bear historical, literary, and gender issues which

Excerpted from "Revolution, Femininity, and Sentimentality in *Billy Budd, Sailor,*" by Cyndy Hendershot, *North Dakota Quarterly,* Winter 1996. Copyright © 1996 by The University of North Dakota. Reprinted with permission.

provide further context for criticism of the work. The novel may be read as a narrative about other texts, as a voyage not on any realistic ocean, but on a textual ocean. Specifically, Melville's novel situates itself in the textual debate over the French Revolution found in Edmund Burke's *Reflections on the Revolution in France* (1790) and Thomas Paine's *The Rights of Man* (1791–92). Billy Budd leaves the ship *The Rights of Man* because of enforced impressment by *The Bellipotent,* a ship whose captain shares the reactionary ideology displayed by Burke in *Reflections.* Melville figures this textual journey through a narrator who is sympathetic to the Burkean view of the Revolution and who, in his narrative, links Billy Budd metaphorically with the Revolution, most strikingly evidenced in the feminization of his character. Although the types of femininities they use are different, both Burke and Melville's narrator trope the Revolution as a feminine threat undermining masculine principles.

BURKE'S *REFLECTIONS*

Edmund Burke's *Reflections on the Revolution in France* frequently feminizes the French Revolution in order to discredit it. Burke genders the supposed rationality and stability of British government as masculine in order to defend its superiority, and conversely he genders the Revolution as feminine in order to discredit it as chaotic and irrational. Burke operates within a binary logic which, [literary critics] Hélène Cixous and Catherine Clément, among others, have argued, characterizes Western thought, a binary logic which privileges masculinity over its inferior and suspect mirror, femininity. Cixous and Clément state that "Philosophy is constructed on the premise of women's abasement. Subordination of the feminine to the masculine order, which gives the appearance of being the condition for the machinery's functioning." In Burke's binary logic Britain displays "a *manly,* moral, regulated liberty" (emphasis added) evidenced in "a *potent* monarchy" (emphasis added) which is characterized by a "more austere and *masculine* morality" (emphasis added). Throughout *Reflections,* Burke uses the assumed superiority of the masculine over the feminine in order to defend British society with its strict hierarchies as the superior system.

Conversely, Burke casts revolutionary France as feminine: France "has abandoned her interest, that she might prostitute her virtue." Specifically, Burke casts the Revolution as a syphilitic whore: "France, when she let loose the reins of regal authority, doubled the license, of a ferocious dissoluteness in manners, and of an insolent irreligion in opinions and practices: and has extended through all ranks of life, as if she were communicating some privilege, or laying open some secluded benefit, all the unhappy corruptions that usually were the disease of wealth and power." In *Reflections,* therefore, Burke discusses the threat of the Revolution to British society as a feminine one, a fallen woman who attempts to seduce the British people away from their "manly" governmental and societal systems.

MELVILLE'S BURKEAN NARRATOR

The narrator of *Billy Budd* employs this same troping of the Revolution as feminine, for Melville creates a narrator in the novel who is sympathetic to the reactionary *Reflections* rather than to *The Rights of Man.* The narrator, like Burke, views the French Revolution and its influences as dangerous and negative. Discussing the Nore Mutiny, caused as he tells us "by live cinders blown across the Channel from France in flames," the narrator states that it is a "contagious fever in a frame constitutionally sound," reminding the reader of Burke's disease metaphors in *Reflections.* Further, the narrator frequently discusses the Revolution in negative feminized metaphorical terms reminiscent of Burke, as, for example, when he refers to the Napoleonic Wars as "a flight of wild harpies [which] rose shrieking from the din and dust of the fallen Bastille." The narrator's valorization of Trafalgar and Nelson further indicates his reactionary view of the Revolution as a danger which threatened British stability.

The narrator's sympathy for Vere serves as further evidence of his Burkean view of the Revolution. Vere's reactionary view, evidenced in his desire to quell the popular threat of Billy Budd by executing him, is supported by the narrator, who sympathizes with Vere and presents his view of the events as truth, a view literalized in the narrator's giving Vere an allegorical name (Vere=Truth). Discussing Vere's view of revolutionary politics, the narrator states that Vere opposes these politics "not alone because they seemed to him insusceptible of embodiment in lasting institutions, but at war with the peace of this world and the true welfare of mankind." This veneration of Vere's view as natural and just coincides with Burke's assertion that the Revolution is "at war with nature." The narrator continually emphasizes his Burkean views through his casting of Vere as the hero of the narrative. Speculating on Billy and Vere's closeted meeting, the narrator states that "it would have been in consonance with the spirit of Captain Vere should he on this occasion have concealed nothing from the condemned one." The narrator manipulates the reader into viewing Vere as truth and hence manipulates him or her into viewing Burkean notions of the French Revolution as truth.

One of the narrator's most striking similarities with Burke

REVOLUTIONARY FRANCE IS DISCREDITED AS FEMININE

Phrased as a letter to a young gentleman in France, this selection from Edmund Burke's Reflections on the Revolution in France *reveals Burke's means of denigrating the revolution by gendering it as feminine. He compares revolutionary France to a licentious woman, and he contrasts revolutionary France with other countries, like England, whose foundations for freedom are religion, manners, and masculine morality.*

Compute your gains: see what is got by those extravagant and presumptuous speculations which have taught your leaders to despise all their predecessors, and all their contemporaries, and even to despise themselves, until the moment in which they became truly despicable. By following those false lights, France has bought undignified calamities at a higher price than any nation has purchased the most unequivocal blessings! France has bought poverty by crime! France has not sacrificed her virtue to her interest; but she has abandoned her interest, that she might prostitute her virtue. All other nations have begun the fabric of a new government, or the reformation of an old, by establishing originally, or by enforcing with greater exactness some rites or other of religion. All other people have laid the foundations of civil freedom in severer manners, and a system of a more austere and masculine morality. France, when she let loose the reins of regal authority, doubled the licence, of a ferocious dissoluteness in manners, and of an insolent irreligion in opinions and practices; and has extended through all ranks of life, as if she were communicating some privilege, or laying open some secluded benefit, all the unhappy corruptions that usually were the disease of wealth and power. This is one of the new principles of equality in France.

Edmund Burke, *Reflections on the Revolution in France* (1790). Ed. Conor Cruise O'Brien. New York: Penguin Books, 1968. Reprinted 1981.

is evidenced in his troping of revolutionary threat as feminine. Billy Budd leaves *The Rights of Man,* bringing with him the threat of revolution that text presents. As will be discussed later, it is the narrator's Burkean conception of a feminized revolutionary force which is at work here, not Paine's actual text, which does not associate the revolution with femininity, but tropes it as masculine.

The narrator, following Burke's binary logic, seeks to discredit Billy's threat by feminizing him. The narrator describes Billy's face as "all but feminine in purity." [Captain] Graveling [on the ship *The Rights of Man*] describes Billy as "the jewel of 'em," associating Billy with female genitalia, an association borne out in the description of him as "the flower of his [the king's] flock," and in the connotations associated with his last name, Budd. Billy is "a rustic beauty transplanted from the provinces and brought into competition with the high born dames of the court." He is like "the beautiful woman in one of Hawthorne's minor tales." After killing Claggart, Billy is like "a condemned vestal priestess." The narrator continually figures Billy's threat to *The Bellipotent* as a feminine one.

In the narrator's version of the story Billy's feminine beauty and sweetness provoke the anger of Claggart and as a result bring the threat of revolution onto the ship, as the popular sailor, Billy, kills his superior, angry and frustrated at the injustice of his accusation. In Billy's trial Vere (who may be seen as a mouthpiece for the narrator's views) makes explicit the danger feminine qualities bring to a rational, "manly" ship. Vere addresses the court, telling them, "let not warm hearts betray heads that should be cool." Read in his statement: let not femininity undermine masculinity, a point Vere makes explicitly when he says, "Ashore in a criminal case, will an upright judge allow himself off the bench to be waylaid by some tender kinswoman of the accused seeking to touch him with her tearful plea? Well, the heart here, sometimes the feminine in man, is as that piteous woman, and hard though it be, she must here be ruled out." Vere makes it clear in this speech that if the feminine is allowed to prevail on *The Bellipotent*, mutiny and chaos will result: give in to the feminine and Burke's syphilitic whore will raise her terrifying head. Vere's execution of Billy violently reinscribes the binary opposition which privileges masculine over feminine.

Billy Budd Is Anti-Homophobic

Kathy J. Phillips

Structuring her article around an honors class discussion of *Billy Budd*, University of Hawaii professor
of English Kathy J. Phillips reveals how her class explored the topic of homosexuality in the novel. In
this selection, Phillips introduces the subject by en-
couraging her students to focus on prohibited speech
in the novel. The discussion then moves to Claggart's
and Vere's homophobia. Phillips concludes the
article with her students' evaluations of two devas-
tating results from repressed sexuality: dehumanizing the enemy and projecting erotic energy into violence and war.

Kathy J. Phillips has published two books, *Virginia Woolf
Against Empire* and *Dying Gods in Twentieth-Century Fiction*, as well as several essays, including "Jane Harrison
and Modernism" and "Exorcising Faustus from Africa."

New readings of *Billy Budd* like Robert Martin's and Eve
Sedgwick's, impossible just a few decades ago, attest to our
present society's at least tentative openness about homosexuality. Reciprocally, *Billy Budd* in the classroom can help
shape a new appreciation of sexual and cultural differences,
based on Melville's own respect, if, as Martin argues, "Melville seriously believed in the radical social potential of male
homosexuality as a force in the creation of a more egalitarian society." One key to such reform might be freer discussion, for when Billy explains why he turned violent, he says
simply, "Could I have used my tongue I would not have
struck him." Extrapolating from Billy's dangerous impediment, I felt that if people could speak more readily about homosexuality and other sexualities, then maybe that exchange of ideas and airing of fears would help abate the
violence—emotional and often physical—of gay bashing. . . .

PROHIBITED SPEECH IN THE PUBLIC AND PRIVATE SPHERES

A list of questions for *Billy Budd* proposed that a major focus of the story is impeded or prohibited speech. I left these terms deliberately ambiguous. If students found homosexuality in the story, some might consider it a forbidden topic, then or now; some might want to talk about it, but feel impeded, fearing that I or their peers might disapprove if they spoke sympathetically. Still others might prefer to keep silent so as not to get jumped on for a negative judgment. When the eight juniors and seniors came to the first of the two discussions on *Billy Budd,* they could very well pinpoint the prohibited public issues. Sailors cannot mention the Nore Mutiny or the grievances that may lead to mutinies, such as the forcible impressment of sailors. Similarly, bluejackets cannot debate the French Revolution or the inequities that may cause peasants to rebel. Nor can soldiers discuss whether a war is just, even (or especially) a war involving themselves.

Melville relates these so-called "public" topics to an apparently "private" sphere in two passages. First, the narrator admits that naval historians sometimes abridge accounts of mutinies at sea, in the same way that an individual "refrains from blazoning aught amiss or calamitous in his family." Although the narrator adds straight-facedly that a historian may hush up mutinies "without reproach," as soon as we looked at the passage, the students began to suspect it of irony. Since Melville *was* reproaching the cover-up of such issues as impressment and war, maybe he was also broaching sensitive "family" topics whose disclosure might have calamitously brought down a label of something "amiss." Second, after commanding Claggart to be direct and say "impressed men," Captain Vere immediately retracts the new frankness; he forbids Claggart to name the mutiny against impressment, because such mention would be "immodest." By introducing a word that usually signals bodies or sex, Melville again seems to be mixing public and private arenas and unsettling their definitions.

To figure out what these "immodest" "family" matters might be and whether they had anything to do with impeded speech, we began to investigate which characters exhibit "tongue-tie." Sam volunteered that a "convulsed tongue-tie" torments Billy, and Tania offered that Claggart also suffers from "lasting tongue-tie." Why? "Because he's dead." "Because he could never admit his feelings toward Billy." Caroline pointed to the scene where Claggart playfully taps Billy from behind with his rattan: "I don't know if I'm the only one to see sexuality here . . ." It's true that modern students are likely to see the word "ejaculate" solely in a sexual context, hardly knowing it once meant "exclaim," but Melville does activate double meanings all along. "Impressed" may mean drafted as well as dazzled at beauty; "consummation" may point to a death and a sexual union. In case anybody missed the sexual connotations or preferred not to consider them, a footnote in the Penguin edition insisted on them by informing us that Titus Oates, whom Claggart is said to resemble, was a seventeenth-century figure accused of being a perjuror as well as a "pervert" with "unnatural vices." Although these words buffet *me*, they're provocative for a class. Some students might be too insulted to speak, some *want* to declaim against "archaic" vocabulary, some say "unnatural" without pausing, some agree to "pervert" but wonder if they'll be "politically incorrect." The official script is likely both to encourage and to incense enough people on either side to keep the discussion going.

CLAGGART'S PHYSICAL AND EMOTIONAL ATTACHMENT

I asked, "Does Melville agree that Claggart in his attraction for Billy is 'unnatural'?" No, Silke recalled, for Melville goes out of his way to make Claggart an example of "Natural Depravity." True, the narrator does include "depravity" in his summation, and we would have to figure out why. Meanwhile, an important point was that Melville subverts the stigma against homoeroticism as "unnatural" (which replaced its earlier stigmatization as "sinful"): [According to a study by John D'Emilio and Estelle B. Freedman] "After the American Revolution, the phrase 'crimes against nature' increasingly appeared in statutes, implying that acts of sodomy offended a natural order rather than the will of God"; in the nineteenth century, the word "sodomy" could refer not only to anal sex between men but also to "various nonprocreative sexual acts, including masturbation and oral sex." For Melville, however, Claggart in his desire for Billy is not unnatural but natural.

In fact, Melville grants Claggart not only a physical attraction, pointedly said to be natural, but also an emotional response, a "soft yearning." Sam introduced into the discussion the officer's "incipient feverish tears" and the key line that "Claggart could even have loved Billy but for fate and ban." We also noted on this same page, "Then would Claggart look like the man of sorrows." Tania, the religion major in the group, recognized the allusion to Christ. Because Melville assigns this allusion frequently to Billy and once to Claggart, and because he gives the affliction of "tongue-tie" to both men, the author sometimes parallels the two. Here the discussion is open to arguments either that their opposition reasserts itself or that the parallels mean Claggart and Billy could have been brothers, not enemies. . . .

If Claggart possesses all that potential to have "loved" Billy, as the narrator speculates, and if that love is "natural," as the narrator further insists, then why does "depravity" cloud the relationship? After all, the narrator informs us that Claggart feels not only attraction but also repulsion toward Billy, "envy and antipathy . . . conjoined like Chang and Eng," Siamese twins. Even this description of Claggart's efforts to push Billy out of his thoughts employs an image of two men in constant physical contact, poignantly emphasizing the difficulty of denying desire. Suppose Claggart were to react to Billy not with hostility but with a "soft yearning" for once undisguised? If we were talking about 1797, when Melville sets the story, Claggart could be hanged, Sam reminded us. He was drawing from his report on [Jeffrey Weeks's article] "The Construction of Homosexuality" the week before: "in February 1816, four members of the crew of the *Africaine* were hanged for buggery. . . . Buggery has been mentioned in the articles of war since the seventeenth century and was treated as seriously as desertion, mutiny or murder." If we thought about Melville's late nineteenth century, we could recall that in England the Labouchère Amendment made "acts of gross indecency" between men punishable by two years' hard labor [according to Weeks] or that, in America, New York law first criminalized consenting sodomy [according to] D'Emilio and Freedman. And if we went on to project Claggart into 1993, the year of our reading, an American Claggart who "came out" in the armed services could be dishonorably discharged.

How does Claggart react under this risk that he could be scorned or even hanged? He resents Billy for putting him in danger, although, as Christopher reminded us, Billy remains oblivious to his erotic effect on others. Claggart paints

Billy to Vere as a "mantrap . . . under the ruddy-tipped daisies"; this charge is either a lie, that Billy is planning a mutiny, or the truth, that Billy has attracted and caught Claggart in a dangerous vulnerability. Claggart's fear of his own homosexual responses and their repercussions causes him to become homophobic, as [Eve Kosofsky] Sedgwick asserts. We stressed in class that it is not homosexuality but homophobia—his society's and Claggart's own internalized version—that makes him destructive. Or, as Melville puts it, if Claggart is "apprehending the good," or what is labeled good, but is "powerless to be it," to conform to the dominant mores, then "what recourse is left" to such a nature, "surcharged with energy . . . but to recoil upon itself and, like the scorpion for which the Creator alone is responsible, act out to the end the part allotted to it . . . ?" Here the discussion could take up the still ongoing debate about whether gays should serve in the military. Does Claggart's case show that they shouldn't? Does repression create violence, recoiled inward and outward? Does the new injunction "Don't ask, don't tell" solve the problem?

HOMOPHOBIA ON THE *BELLIPOTENT*

To see what happens to sexuality under the *Bellipotent*'s rule of homophobia, we looked at the scene of Claggart's accusation and Billy's response. Claggart approaches Billy as an "asylum physician" treats a "patient" beginning to show signs of "a coming paroxysm." He looks at Billy "mesmerically," with "serpent fascination," then lurches out like a "torpedo fish." Melville seems to be drawing on the language offered by the late nineteenth-century "medical model" of homosexuality as a "mental illness," as Sam had reported in his discussion of Weeks['s article]. It wasn't until 1974 that the American Psychiatric Association erased this definition from its list of disorders [D'Emilio and Freedman claim]. . . .

Although the narrator seems to know the medical model for homosexuality, he resists the temptation to classify by insisting that Claggart belongs rather to "certain uncatalogued creatures of the deep." He adds disdainfully that "to draw the exact line of demarcation few will undertake, though for a fee becoming considerate some professional experts will. There is nothing nameable but that some men will, or undertake to, do it for pay." Although the narrator dismisses the labelers, Claggart has apparently internalized their pronouncements. He then projects what he accepts as his own "ill" desires onto Billy and casts himself as the controlling doctor—meanwhile maintaining the close, indeed erotic relationship that psychoanalysts are sometimes suspected of maintaining with patients. The whole scene between "physician" and "patient" becomes a kind of displaced sexual encounter, with the "lurch of the torpedo fish" and the "paroxysm" evoking erection and ejaculation. Yet when the doctor, the military man, the policeman, the upright citizen won't admit their own sexual responses, that energy fuels power, not love. This master at "arms," who could have been a master at embracing and love, becomes instead a master of hating and weaponry. The scene turns from a hinted sexual encounter into a mimed homosexual rape; Billy is said to feel "gagged" and "impaled," as if forcibly engaged in oral sex and sodomy. A "startling impotence" grips Billy because he cannot speak and because all sexual response between potential equals is lost in aggressive power plays. Because of interdiction, his response becomes even more destructive than Claggart's: "quick as the flame from a discharged cannon at night, his right arm shot out . . . the body fell over lengthwise, like a heavy plank tilted from erectness. A gasp or two, and he lay motionless." What could have been a coital gasp signals instead a murder, and what could have been an ejaculation recalls only the discharge of a cannon. Billy's attempt to refute Claggart's accusation does not break ship's rules as much as Vere thinks, because Billy's and Claggart's energies have been displaced already into the action of the cannon. Billy's "private" violence does not so much disrupt as duplicate and prepare for the systemic violence of war. . . .

VERE'S MASKED ATTRACTION AND HOMOPHOBIA

In some ways, Vere displays an attraction to Billy that is more interesting than Claggart's, because even more masked—or so he thinks. Karen noticed that the first time the captain sees Billy, he is already imagining him "in the nude"; Vere thinks of recommending the young man for a job "that would more frequently bring him under his own observation." If Vere is drawn to Billy as Claggart is, why does he kill him? He claims to bypass the usual referral to the admiral because the sailors might interpret a failure to punish Billy's attack as timidity. However, the Articles of War and the Mutiny Act to which

Vere appeals do not really support him. We wondered if Vere's obsession with an "engagement" meant that he dreaded a hostile engagement—a battle at sea which the sailors might refuse to fight—or a loving engagement, a kind of betrothal to Billy. Exactly as in Claggart's case, the ban against such homoerotic bonds produces fear, which in turn generates a need to get rid of the supposed source of desire (actually located in himself). As Tania concluded in a short paper on the novella, Billy is a Christ-figure because Christ is said to have died for others' sins, and Billy dies to eradicate all signs of what Claggart and Vere have been trained to regard as their sin of attraction.

To gain insight into Vere, we free-associated with his name. Lyanne proposed "verity"; Vere is claiming all truth and justice on his side. Caroline suggested "virility"; she came to class before the first discussion with a fine paper questioning "Captain Virility" and his need to reassert his definition of masculinity. What is this definition? First, "real men" can't be attracted to other men, Vere thinks, so he can't acknowledge his physical urges. In this context, he may reveal more than he intends by alluding to Orpheus controlling the beasts. In Ovid's version, Maenads tear Orpheus apart because the women are jealous when Orpheus, after Eurydice's death, sleeps only with boys. Vere might well anticipate that his society would tear him apart if anybody detected in this "bachelor of forty" any desire to touch boy Billy. Moreover, to Vere himself, such sexual desires would be "beastly," just as the peasants across the channel who might demand a more egalitarian economic system would also be beasts, according to his aristocratic upbringing. Ironically, Vere's efforts to avert being labeled a "beast" cause him to become one, savagely destroying Billy. The more Vere tries to correct what he takes to be a "veering" from the "masculine" code, the more he veers from truth—lying to himself—and from justice.

Second, just as Vere cannot admit physical impulses, he cannot accept emotional ones. He rejects emotion because, in typical nineteenth-century fashion, he associates feeling with women. Vere pushes away "the feminine in man," which in context turns out to include the "heart" as well as the "conscience." Tania argued that when Vere climbs "the slant deck . . . against primitive instincts strong as the wind and the sea," he resists both passion and compassion for

Billy, feelings which he stigmatizes as "primitive" as well as "feminine." However, because Melville reverses the usual evaluation of "civilized" over "primitive," longing for an openly sexual, peaceful "Adam before the Fall," we suspected that Melville might also be rehabilitating the "feminine," moving away from its association with "weakness." Karen regretted, however, that Melville could accomplish this subversion only by salvaging a so-called "feminine" side for men, while banishing all live women from the scene. . . .

REPRESSED SEXUALITY FUELS VIOLENCE AND WAR

Trained to define and then shun "effeminacy," Claggart and Vere apparently worry that if they associate with Billy, they too will be seen as feminine. And, as Chris included in his report, "fear of being considered a woman . . . is the sexual underbelly of combat." Why do men panic at being compared to women? Does the aversion to so-called "womanly" traits—to the emotion of what Vere calls the "tearful" woman, for example—reflect some irrational terror of emasculation, as if just by acquiring a few of these imputed traits a man might lose the capacity for orgasm? However, as we saw in [Virginia Woolf's novel] *Orlando,* men have as much inclination to cry as women, and, for all the Victorian characterization of respectable women as "passionless," women do have a physical capacity for orgasm, as men do. Why should men wince at any comparison to women when such similarities already exist? Or is the aversion less an anxiety about losing physical powers and more a nervousness at losing social status? As Lyanne argued, a man playing the role of a woman in 1993 still raises more eyebrows than a woman playing a man: "Who would want to be demoted?"

To see if Vere's haste in executing Billy stems from his fear of his own transgression of what he takes to be virility, we looked at the encounter where he informs Billy of the sentence against him. The narrator conjectures that Billy may have felt "joy," while Vere may have "developed" his latent "passion." Vere may have let himself "melt back" into a "primeval" upwelling of feeling, and he may have "caught Billy to his heart," in the "sacrament" that occurs whenever two of Nature's "nobler order" come together to "embrace." The narrator then pronounces this possible embrace with passion between two men "diviner magnanimity"—an assertion of goodness risky enough in his own day and not entirely safe in all quarters in our own. . . .

Perhaps because Melville's narrator knows some lack of safety in his own day, he reverences Vere's and Billy's "diviner magnanimity" as they embrace, but he finds something ominous shadowing his praise: "There is no telling the sacrament" of their embrace, he says; it took place in "privacy" and "holy oblivion . . . providentially covers all at last." The students interpreted this oblivion as sexual bliss, or a discreet hushing up of anything sexual—or death. In Melville's shrewdest indictment, he warns that if Vere cannot obtain this "holy oblivion" in the form of ecstasy, because his society wouldn't approve such an embrace between men, then he may scramble for it furtively, behind the scenes—or, worse, he may displace that sexuality onto death-dealing. . . .

This channeling of repressed sexuality into war takes two forms in *Billy Budd*. First, learning to deny one's own human responses makes it easier to deny the humanity of so-called enemies. Even when Vere suspects that some of the French conscripts may hold views as monarchic and undemocratic as his own, he can anticipate fighting these men with whom he has no quarrel, simply because he wears the ludicrously trivial "buttons" of Empire. If Vere and his men follow an imperial code that they do not necessarily support, he claims that "we are not responsible." According to an American professor in Europe, German students aware of the Nazi past were particularly attuned to the dangerous implications of Vere's willingness to deny responsibility.

Second, the energy that could express love, once repressed, seems to go on blindly fueling a parody of love. These soldiers *need* war—any war, without asking the cause—because it provides the only intensity they are allowed on that ship. If, as the students said, the name of the ship, *Bellipotent,* suggests "potent," "belligerence," and "belle," then the meaning could slide either toward "the omnipotence of war" or "the potency of the beautiful one." The story devastatingly records how denying Billy's power to arouse the other men erotically plows that energy into the killing fields.

Billy Budd Condemns Capital Punishment

H. Bruce Franklin

In the last decades of the nineteenth century, when Melville was writing *Billy Budd*, debate about capital punishment was raging. According to Rutgers University professor H. Bruce Franklin, such issues as the efficacy of public execution as deterrent, the relative guilt of private criminals acting from passion and the public who condoned planned executions, and the cruelty of death by hanging as opposed to electrocution were hotly debated. However, both opponents and proponents of capital punishment condemned what they called the "Bloody Code" or the "Georgian Code," a list of over one hundred offenses which carried the death penalty in England until the 1880s. This code included fifty crimes that had been punishable by death in England since the seventeenth century and the additional sixty capital crimes added to the list by King George III in the eighteenth century.

In this selection, Franklin reminds readers that Melville set *Billy Budd* in 1797 aboard a British warship. Set during the reign of George III, the code that Vere supports would be the "Bloody Code," which was universally condemned in the late nineteenth century. Franklin also argues that Billy's public execution by hanging as a result of Vere's manipulation of the court raises issues pertinent to the nineteenth-century debate on capital punishment: Is public execution a deterrent? Is hanging cruel and unusual? Is the state that condones public execution more guilty than the private perpetrator of an accidental crime? Franklin concludes that Melville's novel contributes to the late nineteenth-century debate on capital punishment by firmly opposing it.

Excerpted from "*Billy Budd* and Capital Punishment: A Tale of Three Centuries," by H. Bruce Franklin, *American Literature*, June 1997. Copyright © 1997 by Duke University Press. Reprinted with permission.

If *Billy Budd* had been published in 1891, when Melville wrote "End of Book" on the last leaf of the manuscript, few readers at the time could have failed to understand that the debate then raging about capital punishment was central to the story, and to these readers the story's position in that debate would have appeared unequivocal and unambiguous. *Billy Budd* derives in part from the American movement against capital punishment. It dramatizes each of the crucial arguments and concepts of that movement. And it brings into vivid focus the key issues of the contemporaneous debate: Which offenses, if any, should carry the death penalty? Does capital punishment serve as a deterrent to killing or as an exemplary model for killing? What are the effects of public executions? Is hanging a method of execution appropriate to a civilized society? Is an impulsive act of killing by an individual more—or less—reprehensible than the apparently calmly reasoned act of judicial killing? Is capital punishment essentially a manifestation of the power of the state? A ritual sacrifice? An instrument of class oppression? A key component of the culture of militarism? Participants on all sides of the debate seemed to agree on only one thing: that the most appalling moment in the history of capital punishment within modern civilization was the reign of George III in England.

When the officers whom Captain Vere has handpicked for his drumhead court appear reluctant to convict Billy and sentence him to death, Vere forcefully reminds these subordinates that they owe their "'allegiance'" not to "'Nature,'" their "'hearts,'" or their "'private conscience,'" but entirely to "'the King'" and his "'imperial [conscience] formulated in the code under which alone we officially proceed.'" The time is 1797, the king is George III, and the code to which Vere refers was known in the nineteenth century as the "Bloody Code."

GEORGE III'S "BLOODY CODE"

During the reigns of the Tudors and Stuarts, fifty crimes had carried the death penalty, and more were slowly added. The most spectacular increase came later, during the reign of George III, when sixty offenses were appended to the death-penalty statutes. By the last third of the nineteenth century, George III's Bloody Code had been universally repudiated and condemned, both in England and America. As the battle against capital punishment raged while Melville was composing *Billy Budd*, partisans on both sides agreed that eliminating most of the code's capital offenses constituted one of the century's notable achievements in human progress. Not surprisingly, opponents of the death penalty cited the Georgian code as barbaric and anachronistic, even for the eighteenth century. For example, a widely reprinted 1889 article [by B. Paul Neuman] referred to "Georgian justice" as "a scandal to the rest of the civilized world," and agreed with [Honoré Gabriel Riqueti] Mirabeau's verdict at the time that "'The English nation is the most merciless of any that I have heard or read of.'" Even advocates of capital punishment celebrated the progress away from the Bloody Code, pointing out that by the early 1880s capital offenses in England had been reduced to "three classes" of deliberate murder, none of which included "crimes committed under circumstances of great excitement, sudden passion, or provocation" [in the words of Samuel Hand]. Articles favoring capital punishment published during the late 1880s argued that the death penalty should certainly "be restricted to murder committed with malice prepense, by a sane person, in resisting arrest, or in the commission of another felony" [as J.M. Buckley says]. Billy Budd, remember, is charged not with murder but with striking "'his superior in grade'"; "'Apart from its effect the blow itself is,'" as Captain Vere states, "'a capital crime'" under the Articles of War of the Georgian code. Nobody on the ship believes the sailor acted with premeditation or malicious—much less murderous—intent, but Vere instructs the court that they must disregard all questions of intent. . . .

THE ISSUE OF PUBLIC HANGINGS

Public execution and hanging, which are integral to Captain Vere's arguments for the necessity of killing Billy Budd, played a complex role in the debates of the last third of the nineteenth century. As abolitionists emphasized the grotesque and sordid spectacles of public hangings, they often played into the hands of retentionists, who saw that their best strategy for preserving the death penalty lay in cleansing it of the features almost universally condemned as loathsome remnants of a savage past.

Between 1833 and 1849, fifteen states abolished public executions, and the movement to banish the practice altogether was unstoppable in the postwar decades. From the late 1860s through the end of the century, hanging became the focal point of abolitionist and reformist arguments, and New York

State became the pivotal battleground. In his 1869 *Putnam's* article "The Gallows in America," Edmund Clarence Stedman (who was to become Melville's most enthusiastic patron during the period of *Billy Budd*'s composition) dwells on the horrors of hanging to convince readers, especially in New York, to abolish the death penalty entirely. . . .

THE HANGING OF BILLY

Although Melville's contemporaries, who almost universally abhorred hanging, might have shuddered at Captain Vere's instantaneous decision that Billy "'must hang,'" the story is carefully crafted to keep the *means* of execution from being a significant issue.

When he is hanged, Billy evinces none of the hideous agonies familiar to the crowds at public hangings and described with sickening detail in countless nineteenth-century essays and books. There is not even the almost invariable muscular spasm or involuntary ejaculation. Chapter 26, obtrusively inserted between Billy's transcendent death and the sailors' reaction, is devoted to a discussion of this perfect lack of motion. The purser suggests that this "'singularity'" must be attributed to Billy's "'will power.'" In the surgeon's response we can hear a parody of the debate transpiring in Melville's New York about the most humane and scientific way to kill a person: "'In a hanging scientifically conducted—and under special orders I myself directed how Budd's was to be effected—any movement following the complete suspension and originating in the body suspended, such movement indicates mechanical spasm in the muscular system. Then the absence of that is no more attributable to will power, as you call it, than to horsepower.'" Admitting to the purser that this "'muscular spasm'" is almost "'invariable,'" the surgeon acknowledges "'I do not, with my present knowledge, pretend to account'" for its absence: "'Even should we assume the hypothesis that at the first touch of the halyards the action of Budd's heart, intensified by extraordinary emotion at its climax, abruptly stopped—much like a watch when in carelessly winding it up you strain at the finish, thus snapping the chain—even under that hypothesis how account for the phenomenon that followed?'"

The purser then asks, "'was the man's death effected by the halter, or was it a species of euthanasia?'" "'*Euthana-*

sia,'" replies the surgeon, has dubious "'authenticity as a scientific term.'" Though it may outwardly resemble the "euthanasia" the *New York Times* had erroneously predicted for electrocution, Billy's death by hanging clearly transcends not only the surgeon's scientific understanding but also the debate about the modalities of capital punishment swirling around the composition of the story.

ACCIDENTAL KILLING VS. STATE EXECUTION

More profoundly relevant to *Billy Budd* are the terms of the debate about the fundamental issue of capital punishment itself. Indeed, the essence of the issue structures the story.

We witness two killings aboard H.M.S. *Bellipotent.* One comes from the impulsive, involuntary fatal blow Billy Budd strikes to the forehead of Claggart. The blow is partly in response to Captain Vere's exhortation to the stammering Billy, "'Defend yourself!'" Vere recognizes that Claggart has been "'Struck dead by an angel of God!'" and he and his drumhead court all acknowledge that Billy acted without malice, forethought, or any murderous intent. The other killing is carried out under cover of law, after reasoned argumentation, and by the state acting through the agency of Captain Vere and his officers.

Which of these two acts constitutes murder? Budd is not even accused of murder. One question that underlies the twentieth-century discussion of *Vere's* act might be framed this way: Does it conform to the 1794 Pennsylvania definition of murder in the "first degree," that is, "wilful, deliberate and premeditated killing"?

And this is precisely how the argument against capital punishment was framed during the years Melville was writing. The fact that hangings were conducted by the state under cover of law did not, to opponents of the death penalty, absolve them from being murders. Indeed, the terms widely used for these killings were "legal murders," "legal killing," and "murder by law." The following commentaries [by Benjamin O. Flower], published in 1890, could apply directly to the two killings on the *Bellipotent*:

> [W]hen a criminal is judged, all the extenuating circumstances shall be taken into consideration. Were this rule observed, the victim of the law would seldom appear in so bad a light as the government that passed the sentence. Let me illustrate the thought: a man commits a murder: the govern-

ment in turn sentences the man to death. Here we have two parties who have presumed to take a human life. . . . the question now arises, upon the shoulders of which party rests the greatest guilt? A most solemn thought. There are many extenuating circumstances in the first instance, but what can be said in justification of the government?

[C]apital punishment administered in any form is essentially a relic of a barbarous age. . . . [T]he State always acts with coolness and deliberation, while ninety per cent. of her children slay their fellowmen in the frenzy of passion.

VERE SUPPORTS GEORGE III'S "BLOODY CODE"

Although Captain Vere has already decided that Billy "'must hang'" before he convenes his drumhead court, the three officers he handpicks are quite reluctant to convict and sentence the Handsome Sailor. In the trial, during which Vere acts as sole witness, prosecutor, and, ultimately, commander of the jury, he finds it necessary to overwhelm his three subordinates with a deluge of arguments. One is precisely that they must "'let not warm hearts betray heads that should be cool.'"

Vere makes his first argument while still in his role of witness (though later he tells the officers, "'Hitherto I have been but the witness, little more'"): "'Quite aside from any conceivable motive actuating the master-at-arms, and irrespective of the provocation to the blow, a martial court must needs in the present case confine its attention to the blow's consequence, which consequence justly is to be deemed not otherwise than as the striker's deed.'" By arguing, especially in such legalistic phraseology, that his court is *not* to consider extenuating circumstances or motive, Vere is underlining for readers in 1891 the fundamental injustice of the proceedings. The three officers, in fact, are disturbed by this manifestation of "a prejudgment on the speaker's part." Later Vere reiterates, "'Budd's intent or non-intent is nothing to the purpose.'"

As discussed earlier, Vere's extended argument that the officers owe their allegiance not to "'Nature,'" their "'hearts,'" or their "'private conscience,'" but entirely to King George III and his "'code under which alone we officially proceed'" would to any late–nineteenth-century audience be an emphatic reminder of the barbaric Bloody Code for which Vere is acting as agent. Vere insists, in fact, that he and his officers must act *merely* as agents and instruments of that law: "'For the law and the rigor of it, we are not responsible. Our vowed responsibility is in this: That however pitilessly that law may operate in any instances, we nevertheless adhere to it and administer it.'" To late–nineteenth-century readers, this would serve as a conspicuous reminder of the horrors of Georgian justice from which nine decades of reform had liberated both the United States and Britain. Each of Vere's arguments, in fact, defends one or more of the most egregious features of the Georgian code, features that had been repudiated by law in those nine ensuing decades.

Immediately after insisting that his officers may not consider "'Budd's intent or non-intent,'" Vere claims that they are taking too much time (a blatantly specious argument, especially in light of the time later spent in the execution and burial rituals): "'strangely we prolong proceedings that should be summary—the enemy may be sighted and an engagement result. We must do; and one of two things must we do—condemn or let go.'" In response, the sailing master, the one trial officer who had not previously spoken, asks "falteringly," "'Can we not convict and yet mitigate the penalty?'"

Insisting that this would not be "'lawful,'" Vere highlights for readers one of the most universally condemned aspects of the code under which he operates: *mandatory* death penalties. Opponents of capital punishment of course focused on the inflexible brutality and cruelty thus codified into law and passing for justice. Joining them, however, were some of the most ardent defenders of capital punishment, including many judges and district attorneys, who were continually encountering juries that—like the sailing master—would rather acquit than consign a criminal to death. In the period from 1860 to 1895, eighteen states shifted from mandatory to discretionary capital punishment, with legislators usually citing the reluctance of juries to participate in capital punishment.

At this point in the trial, Vere abruptly shifts from all his previous arguments—which were based on the premise that he and his drumhead court *must*, under law, sentence Billy to death—to the argument that finally convinces his officers: they *should* hang Billy in a public execution. "His closing appeal," the narrator informs us, is not to their reason but "to their *instinct* as sea officers" (italics mine), and this is what makes it so convincing—at least to them.

This appeal is based solely on the doctrine of deterrence,

the main argument preserving capital punishment through-out the nineteenth (as well as the twentieth) century. By the late 1880s, however, vast amounts of statistical and other evidence had demonstrated that there is little if any reasonable basis for the belief that capital punishment deters any of the crimes for which it is imposed. Nevertheless, the defenders of capital punishment, like Vere, tended more and more to abandon the argument that it was just, fair, appropriate, ordained by God, et cetera, and more and more to rely on belief in its value as a deterrent to crime. They appealed not so much to evidence as to the fear of violent crime widespread among the privileged and affluent classes, a fear which they of course encouraged.

Like the typical nineteenth-century defender of capital punishment, Vere appeals to the fear of the fellow members of his privileged class on the *Bellipotent,* in other words to "their instinct as sea officers." There is, however, one fundamental difference between the deterrence argument familiar to nineteenth-century readers and Vere's decisive argument. The customary argument was (and is) that capital punishment deters the particular crime by making an example of the criminal. Vere's argument—far more cynical—is that hanging Billy Budd before the crew will intimidate them and reinforce the "'arbitrary discipline'" exerted over them by the officers, while *not* hanging him would encourage mutiny. Mutiny is the crime of which Claggart had falsely accused Billy and of which Vere and his officers know Billy is innocent. But, argues Vere, "'the people,'" because they "'have not that kind of intelligent responsiveness that might qualify them to comprehend and discriminate,'" will believe that Billy has committed "'a flagrant act of mutiny'" and will therefore emulate him if he is not appropriately punished for it. For readers in 1891, Vere's argument, so persuasive to his subordinate officers, would seem so obviously specious and illogical as to appear virtually a parody of the usual defense of capital punishment for the sake of deterrence. . . .

MELVILLE CONDEMNS THE ARTICLES OF WAR

There remains a question that by now must have occurred to most readers of this essay: Do not military circumstances, especially during war, demand the kind of martial law under which Vere proceeds (or claims to proceed)? A book published in 1850 presented in chapter after chapter a detailed refutation of this position. Ascribing British naval law of this period to a "barbarous feudal aristocracy" that had regained power in the Restoration and its sequel, the author argued that in the Interregnum, "a period deemed so glorious to the British Navy, these Articles of War were unknown." Therefore, he reasoned, "such tyrannical ordinances are not indispensable—even during war—to the highest possible efficiency of a military marine." He pointed out that Nelson (lionized in *Billy Budd*) opposed corporal punishment and routinely reassigned "wholly ungovernable" seamen to an admiral who "held in abhorrence all corporal punishment," thereby winning the loyalty of these men. "The mutinous effects of government abuses in the Navy," according to this writer, "developed themselves at the great mutiny of the Nore." The author summed up his view in these words:

> Certainly the necessities of navies warrant a code for its government more stringent than the law that governs the land; but that code should conform to the spirit of the political institutions of the country that ordains it. It should not convert into slaves some of the citizens of a nation of freemen.

He then denounced the American Articles of War as "an importation from abroad, even from Britain, whose laws we Americans hurled off as tyrannical, and yet retained the most tyrannical of all." That author, of course, was Herman Melville. The book was *White-Jacket*, a volume he consulted frequently while composing *Billy Budd* on a writing box to which he had glued the motto: "Keep true to the dreams of thy youth."

APPENDIX

THE ROYAL NAVY CIRCA 1797

Throughout *Billy Budd*, much is made of the type of ships involved in any given action. Below are several specific descriptions of the vessels to which Melville refers.

Brig: A Brig is a two-masted vessel, square-rigged—i.e. a vessel with yards and sails set across the masts as opposed to a fore-and-aft rigged craft—on both masts.

Frigate: A fast, three masted fully rigged ship of the fifth or sixth rate (i.e. carrying anywhere from 20 to 48 guns). At the time of this narrative, frigates served primarily "scouts" for the main body of the fleet.

Ironclads: Generally, the term applies to all ships clad with iron for defense. At the time of the narrative, however, there had been no large-scale development for protecting ships in this way. It is the gradual improvement of artillery during the 18th century that laid the foundation for the emergence of the ironclad in the 19th century.

Line-of-Battle-Ships: Broadly, any rated ship of sufficient size to take part in the battle line during a major fleet action.

Rate: Rate applies to the classification of ships according to size and armament. There were six rates at the time of the narrative: 1st (100+ guns), 2nd (90–98 guns), 3rd (64–80 guns), 4th (50–60 guns), 5th (32–48 guns), and 6th (20–32 guns). Ships of the first three rates were considered powerful enough to fight in a line of battle in a major fleet action.

Man-of-War: Any armed ship of a national navy usually carrying between 20 and 120 guns.

"Seventy-four": A third rate man-of-war carrying seventy-four guns. The seventy-four, the type of ship that made up the bulk of the royal fleet at the time of the narrative, was noted for the balance of firepower and maneuverability.

Squadron: In the most general sense, a squadron is any detachment of warships on some special duty. In the British Navy, it was one of three divisions—the red, blue, or white—of the fleet forming one body under the command of a flag-officer.

Steamer: As opposed to a Steamboat, a light-draft vessel used in inland waters, a Steamship is a fully-armed sea-going ship powered by steam as opposed to sail.

Three-deckers: More than simply a ship with three decks, it is a ship fitted for carrying guns on three decks. The *Indomitable* [called *Bellipotent* in the standard transcription] is a seventy-four gun two decker ship; larger ships such as Nelson's first-rater H.M.S. *Victory* were three deckers.

HIERARCHY AT SEA

Commissioned Officers: At the top of the naval military hierarchy, the commissioned officers are those who hold, in writing, a warrant or letters patent issued by the state that grant authority to hold office and exercise duties.

> Admiral: The highest naval officer of flag-rank who commands one of the principal divisions of the fleet. Depending on which division he commands (van or fore, middle, or rear), the admiralty is divided into positions of Admiral, Vice-Admiral, and Rear-Admiral.

> Captain: In the navy, the Captain holds the commissioned rank next below rear-admiral. By extension, the term is applied to a commander of any naval vessel, regardless of commissioned rank.

> First Officer or First Mate: The commissioned officer next in rank to the master of the ship.

> First Lieutenant, Lieutenants: The most junior of the traditional officers' naval ranks. Though the terminology had shifted a bit by Melville's time, at the time of the narrative, the first lieutenant was an executive officer of the marines charged with stationing officers and crew for the necessary handling of the sails, at the guns, and in the messes. The Lieutenants hold rank equal to that of Captain in the army and are charged primarily with duty as watch-officers, i.e. serving as the representative of the commanding officer while on duty.

> Chaplain: Though he could also be appointed as an inferior officer, the Chaplain was often a commissioned officer of rank. Regardless of rank, the Chaplain's duties included those that his corollary on land would serve: preaching, ministering to the sick, and counseling the condemned.

Wardroom or Warrant Officers: One of a varied group of officers below the commissioned officers. They served as heads of specialized technical branches of the ships' company.

> Purser: Appointed by admiralty warrant but having no professional examination, the purser was responsible for keeping the ship's accounts and for issuing provisions and clothing. By the beginning of the nineteenth century, the purser was considered a wardroom officer.

Sailing Master: The officer charged with navigation of the ship.

Surgeon: A member of the medical detachment aboard a ship. Generally, he was prevented from involvement in conflicts, instead serving within the hold to help treat those injured.

Midshipman: Non-commissioned sea-officers who were considered prospective commissioned officers. One in such a position would, after two years of service, take an examination to be commissioned as a lieutenant.

Rate: For titles of station aboard a ship, all non-commissioned officers were marked in the ship's muster-book according to skills and duties. The chief grades in the Royal Navy were seaman (subdivided into ordinary and able), petty officers, and landsmen. The term also applies to the classification of ships according to size and armament.

Petty Officers: Simply a naval officer corresponding in rank to a non-commissioned officer in the army. He holds position at the discretion and pleasure of the appointing authority, generally the commanding officer.

Boatswain: Usually one of the best sailors, the boatswain (pronounced 'bosun') was responsible for inspecting the ship's sails and rigging every morning. He was also in charge of all deck activities, such as dropping anchor and handling the sails. He issued orders piping on a silver boatswain's whistle.

Apothecary: Appointed by the surgeon of the cruise, he is the chief assistant to the medical officer.

Armorer: The petty officer in charge of keeping the small-arms in condition for service.

Captain of the Hold: In this sense, Captain refers to a specific leading man of the ship's company charged with maintaining order in the portion of the ship below the lower deck.

Corporal: In this case the ship's Corporal who assists the Master-at-Arms with his duties.

Coxswain: The person who has charge of the boat and crew in the absence of officers. On a man-of-war, the Captain's coxswain ranked high among the petty officers and had charge of the Captain's boat and attends him.

Master-at-Arms, "Jimmy Legs": The chief petty officer aboard a man-of-war, the Master-at-Arms (as Melville notes) attends to the police duties of the ship. The title derives from his traditional duty of instructing the crew in the use of small arms. "Jimmy Legs" is a humorous nickname for the Master-at-Arms.

Ship's Yeoman: An appointed officer who has charge of stores and keeps accounts in his special department.

Marines, Marine Guard: As distinguished from sailors, the

marines where specialized soldiers who served aboard a man-of-war. During the time of the narrative, a large ship of line like the seventy-four often consisted of more than twenty percent marines who served in gun crews, with boarding parties, and as sharp-shooters or sentries.

Captain of the Marines: Though under the broad control of the naval admiralty, the Captain of the Marines, the ranking marine aboard a man-of-war, was responsible for command over the marines while under sail.

Sailors, Bluejackets: As opposed to marines, the terms used in reference to all experienced, skilled seaman. The term 'bluejacket' derived from the color of their uniform.

Helmsman: the sailor charged with piloting the ship.

Landsmen: As opposed to skilled seaman, the landsmen were those with no naval training who performed basic tasks on ship such as hauling and hoisting.

Afterguard, Afterguardsmen: The afterguardsmen, usually drawn from the landsmen who are not required to go aloft except to loose and furl the mainsail, are those stationed on the quarter-deck and poop to man the gear. . . .

SAILS

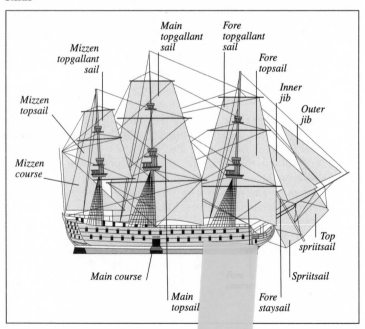

Mainmast, Mainmastmen: The c   st in a three-masted ship. The mainmastmen are those   ties involve working with that mast.

Mizzenmast: On a three-masted ship, the rear mast most aft near the stern.

Masthead: The masthead is the highest reach of the mast where the flag is flown. More specifically, the term refers to the head of the lower mast used for observation or a place of confinement as punishment.

Spar: A spar is the general term for all the poles in a vessels rigging and includes masts, yards, and booms.

Tops, Topmen: The top is, appropriately, the top of the mast and the small platform there. The various tops are named for the mast on which they sit (foretop, maintop, etc.). Those who are stationed for duty in the tops are topmen.

> Foretop, Foretopmen: The top of the foremast. Generally, the foretopmen were younger, stronger seamen.

> Mizzentop, Mizzentopmen: The aft-most top. The mizzentopmen were usually older, more experienced sailors a bit past their prime and less fit for service in the fore or main top.

Shrouds: A range of large ropes extending from the mastheads to the sides of the ship to provide lateral support to the masts thereby enabling them to carry the sails. Parallel bands of ratlines between the shrouds functioned as ladders for the topmen to climb up and down the mastheads.

Yards, Yardarm: A yard is the long, narrow wooden spar slung at its center from the mast and serving to support and extend a square sail that is bent into it. The yardarm is either of the ends of the yard. It is from these that men were hanged. (as with most things on a ship, the yards are identified by the position and mast). . . .

DECKS

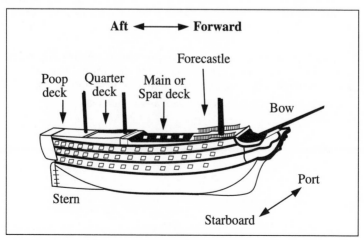

Forecastle, Forecastlemen: The short raised deck at the fore of the ship originally used by archers. In a man-of-war, it is the upper part of the deck forward of the foremast. The term forecastlemen refers to any member of the crew whose quarters were beneath that deck. . . .

Poop-deck: A partial deck which is the portion of the spar-deck extending from the mizzenmast aft.

Quarter-deck, Quarter-deck Cabin: The part of the spar-deck from the mainmast aft. It is generally reserved for commanding officers and the officer of the deck. . . .

OTHER USEFUL TERMS

Batteries: Any place where the guns and mortar are mounted. The term is also used to designate collectively a body of cannon. . . .

Watch, Dog-watch: The watch is the period of time that each division of the ship's company alternately remains on deck. A watch lasts for four hours, with the exception of the dog-watch which lasts two and serves to prevent the watch from being kept by the same men every day. The various watches are: First (2000 to midnight); Middle or Graveyard (midnight to 0400); Morning (0400 to 0800); Forenoon (0800 to 1200); Afternoon (1200 to 1600); First Dog (1600 to 1800); and Second Dog (1800 to 2000). . . .

Drumhead, Drumhead Court: The Drumhead itself is the circular top of the capstan where the bars are fitted to aid in turning. The Drumhead Court, a summary court martial held while the ship is still at sea and presided over by the ranking officer, takes its name from the occasional necessity of the drumhead doing service as a writing table. Usually, only the senior naval officers—as opposed to marine officers—make up the court which has full power to convict and sentence while at sea. . . .

Mess, Messmates: Each mess designates the specific divisions of a company of officers or crew who take their meals together in a given place. Those members of the same mess are termed messmates.

Muster: As a verb, to muster is to assemble the entire ship's company for an inspection, exercise, or other communal activity. As a noun, the muster is a list of the members of the ship's company.

From the University of Virginia website, http://xroads.virginia.edu.

CHRONOLOGY

1819

Herman Melville is born to Allan and Maria Melville in New York City on August 1.

1830

The Melville family moves to Albany.

1832

Melville's father, Allan, dies. Melville leaves school to work as a clerk in the bank in Albany. His mother, Maria, moves the rest of the family to Pittsfield, Massachusetts, to the farm of Thomas Melville.

1837

Melville goes to Pittsfield to run his uncle's farm; his uncle, Thomas Melville, goes to Galena, Illinois. In the fall, Melville teaches at a rural school near Pittsfield.

1838

Melville takes a course in surveying and engineering at Lansingburgh Academy in New York, hoping to be employed by the Erie Canal Engineering Department.

1839

When Melville is not hired by the Erie Canal Engineering Department, he signs on as a common sailor on the merchant ship *St. Lawrence*, bound for Liverpool, England. When he returns from the four-month voyage, he teaches school at Greenbush, near Albany. Melville later bases his novel *Redburn* on this voyage.

1840

Melville travels to Galena, Illinois, to visit his uncle. He will later use this experience in his novel *The Confidence-Man*.

1841

Melville sets sail on the whaler *Acushnet* on January 3.

1842

Melville and Richard T. Greene desert the *Acushnet* on July 9. Melville lives with the Typee tribe for a month. On August 9, he signs aboard the Australian whaler *Lucy Ann*. On September 20, he refuses duty when docked in Tahiti and is imprisoned briefly. After wandering around the islands for a month, he signs on the Nantucket whaler *Charles and Henry*. Melville uses his experiences among the Typee tribe in his first novel, *Typee*. His second novel, *Omoo*, is loosely based on his ramblings around Tahiti. His experiences aboard all three whaling ships are evidenced in his sixth novel, *Moby-Dick*. Three men, Philip Spencer, Elisha Small, and Samuel Cromwell, are accused of mutiny on the brig *Somers;* they are hanged on December 1.

1843

In May, Melville is discharged in Hawaii. He works in Honolulu until August, then joins the navy and boards the frigate *United States*. Melville's novel *White-Jacket* is loosely based on this voyage.

1844

Melville is discharged from the navy in early October.

1846

Melville's first novel, *Typee*, is published in both England and America.

1847

Omoo is published. Melville marries Elizabeth Shaw on August 4.

1849

Malcolm Melville is born on February 16. Melville publishes *Mardi* and *Redburn*.

1850

White-Jacket is published. Melville moves his family to Pittsfield, Massachusetts, and buys a farm they name Arrowhead. He meets Nathaniel Hawthorne and writes a review of his work, "Hawthorne and His Mosses." He works steadily on *Moby-Dick*. Melville's father-in-law, Judge Lemuel Shaw, is involved in two controversial court cases, one involving returning a fugitive slave and one a homicide trial.

1851

Moby-Dick is published in England and America. Stanwix Melville is born on October 22.

1852

Melville's seventh novel, *Pierre: or the Ambiguities,* is published.

1853

Elizabeth (Bessie) Melville is born on May 22. Melville writes *The Isle of the Cross,* which is never published and is perhaps destroyed. He also writes stories for *Putnam's* and *Harper's* monthly magazines.

1854

Israel Potter is published serially in *Putnam's.*

1855

Frances (Fanny) Melville is born on March 2. *Israel Potter* is published in book form.

1856

The Piazza Tales, which include "Bartleby, the Scrivener" and "Benito Cereno," is published. Melville works on *The Confidence-Man.*

1856–1857

Melville sails to Europe and the Holy Land. This journey finds its way into Melville's long poem, *Clarel.*

1857

The Confidence-Man is published in London and New York.

1857–1860

Melville lectures in the Northeast and Midwest on "Statues in Rome," "The South Seas," and "Travel."

1861

Melville goes to Washington to seek a naval appointment when the Civil War begins. His father-in-law, Judge Lemuel Shaw, dies suddenly of a stroke.

1863

The Melvilles move from Pittsfield, Massachusetts, back to New York City.

1864

Melville visits the Virginia battlefields.

1866

Melville's collection of Civil War poems, *Battle-Pieces,* is published. He is appointed assistant inspector at the New York Custom House.

1867

Melville's son Malcolm dies of a self-inflicted gunshot wound.

1876

Melville's eighteen-thousand-line poem, *Clarel*, is published.

1880

Melville's daughter Frances marries Henry B. Thomas.

1882

Eleanor Melville Thomas is born.

1885

On December 31, Melville retires from his position at the New York Custom House.

1886

Melville's son Stanwix dies on February 23 of tuberculosis. Melville is working on three collections of poems and his final short novel, *Billy Budd*.

1888

Melville privately publishes *John Marr and Other Sailors*.

1891

Melville privately publishes *Timoleon*. He is preparing his third collection of poems, *Weeds and Wildings*, for publication and he is revising *Billy Budd* when he dies on September 28.

1924

Billy Budd is transcribed by Raymond Weaver and published.

1948

F. Barron Freeman attempts a definitive text of *Billy Budd*.

1962

Harrison Hayford and Merton M. Sealts Jr. complete a new transcription of the manuscript and publish the now standard edition of *Billy Budd, Sailor*.

For Further Research

Melville's Works of Special Interest

Herman Melville, *Billy Budd, Sailor (An Inside Narrative)*. Ed. by Harrison Hayford and Merton M. Sealts Jr. Chicago: University of Chicago Press, 1962.

——, *Collected Poems of Herman Melville*. Ed. Howard P. Vincent. Chicago: Packard, 1947.

——, *Moby-Dick*. Ed. Harrison Hayford and Hershel Parker. New York and London: W.W. Norton, 1967.

——, *White-Jacket, or the World in a Man-of-War*. New York: Grove Press, 1959.

About Melville

The Heath Anthology of American Literature. Vol. 1. Lexington, MA: D.C. Heath, 1990.

Tyrus Hillway, *Herman Melville*. New York: Twayne, 1963.

Leon Howard, *Herman Melville: A Biography*. Berkeley and Los Angeles: University of California Press, 1951.

David Kirby, *Herman Melville*. New York: Continuum, 1993.

Jay Leyda, *The Melville Log: A Documentary Life of Herman Melville, 1819–1891*. 2 vols. New York: Harcourt, Brace, 1951.

Eleanor Melville Metcalf, *Herman Melville: Cycle and Epicycle*. Cambridge, MA: Harvard University Press, 1953.

Hershel Parker, *Herman Melville: A Biography*. Baltimore, MD: Johns Hopkins University Press, 1996.

Laurie Robertson-Lorant, *Melville: A Biography*. New York: Clarkson Potter, 1996.

Leonard Unger, ed., *American Writers: A Collection of Literary Biographies*. Vol. 3. New York: Scribners, 1974.

Raymond M. Weaver, *Herman Melville: Mariner and Mystic.* New York: George H. Doran, 1921.

ABOUT MELVILLE'S WORKS

Watson G. Branch, ed., *Melville: The Critical Heritage.* London and Boston: Routledge and Kegan Paul, 1974.

John Bryant, ed., *A Companion to Melville Studies.* New York: Greenwood Press, 1986.

———, *The Evermoving Dawn: Essays in Celebration of the Melville Centennial.* Kent, OH: Kent State University Press, 1996.

H. Bruce Franklin, *The Wake of the Gods: Melville's Mythology.* Stanford, CA: Stanford University Press, 1963.

Kathleen E. Kier, *The Melville Encyclopedia: The Novels.* Troy, NY: Whitston, 1990.

A. Robert Lee, ed., *Herman Melville: Reassessments.* London and Totawa, NJ: Vision Press and Barnes & Noble Books, 1984.

Robert K. Martin, *Hero, Captain, and Stranger: Male Friendship, Social Critique, and Literary Form in the Sea Novels of Herman Melville.* Chapel Hill: University of North Carolina Press, 1986.

Martin Leonard Pops, *The Melville Archetype.* Kent, OH: Kent State University Press, 1970.

Faith Pullin, ed., *New Perspectives on Melville.* Kent, OH: Kent State University Press, 1978.

Michael Paul Rogin, *Subversive Genealogy: The Politics and Art of Herman Melville.* New York: Alfred A. Knopf, 1983.

Thomas J. Rountree, ed., *Critics on Melville.* Coral Gables, FL: University of Miami Press, 1972.

Eve Kosofsky Sedgwick, *Epistomology of the Closet.* Berkeley and Los Angeles: University of California Press, 1990.

William Ellery Sedgwick, *Herman Melville: The Tragedy of Mind.* New York: Russell & Russell, 1962.

John Seelye, *Melville: The Ironic Diagram.* Evanston, IL: Northwestern University Press, 1970.

Rowland A. Sherrill, *The Prophetic Melville: Experience, Transcendence, and Tragedy.* Athens: University of Georgia Press, 1979.

Christopher Sten, ed., *Savage Eye: Melville and the Visual Arts*. Kent, OH: Kent State University Press, 1991.

Milton R. Stern, *The Fine Hammered Steel of Herman Melville*. Urbana: University of Illinois Press, 1957.

Lawrance Thompson, *Melville's Quarrel with God*. Princeton, NJ: Princeton University Press, 1952.

ABOUT *BILLY BUDD*

Joseph Allen Boone, "Male Independence and the American Quest Romance as Counter-Traditional Genre: Hidden Sexual Politics," *Tradition Counter Tradition*. Chicago: University of Chicago Press, 1987.

Gail Coffler, "Classical Iconography in the Aesthetics of *Billy Budd, Sailor*," *Savage Eye: Melville and the Visual Arts*. Ed. Christopher Sten. Kent, OH: Kent State University Press, 1991.

Richard Harter Fogle, "*Billy Budd*: The Order of the Fall," *Nineteenth-Century Fiction*, vol. 15, 1960–1961.

H. Bruce Franklin, "*Billy Budd* and Capital Punishment: A Tale of Three Centuries," *American Literature*, June 1997.

Stanton Garner, "Fraud and Fact in Herman Melville's *Billy Budd*," *San Jose Studies*, vol. 4, no. 4, 1978.

Peter L. Hays and Richard Dilworth Rust, "'Something Healing': Fathers and Sons in *Billy Budd*," *Nineteenth-Century Fiction*, December 1979.

Cyndy Hendershot, "Revolution, Femininity, and Sentimentality in *Billy Budd, Sailor*," *North Dakota Quarterly*, Winter 1996.

Richard A. Hocks, "Melville and 'The Rise of Realism': The Dilemma of History in *Billy Budd*," *American Literary Realism*, Winter 1994.

Barbara Johnson, "Melville's Fist: The Execution of *Billy Budd*," *Studies in Romanticism*, Winter 1979.

C.N. Manlove, "Organic Hesitancy: Theme and Style in *Billy Budd*," *New Perspectives on Melville*. Ed. Faith Pullin. Kent, OH: Kent State University Press, 1978.

James McIntosh, "*Billy Budd, Sailor*: Melville's Last Romance," *Critical Essays on Melville's* Billy Budd, Sailor. Ed. Robert Milder. Boston: G.K. Hall, 1989.

Robert Milder, ed., *Critical Essays on Melville's* Billy Budd, Sailor. Boston: G.K. Hall, 1989.

Hershel Parker, *Reading* Billy Budd. Evanston, IL: Northwestern University Press, 1990.

Kathy J. Phillips, "*Billy Budd* as Anti-Homophobic Text," *College English*, December 1994.

Thomas J. Scorza, *In the Time Before Steamships:* Billy Budd *and the Limits of Politics and Modernity*. DeKalb: Northern Illinois University Press, 1979.

Merton M. Sealts Jr., "Innocence and Infamy: *Billy Budd, Sailor*," *A Companion to Melville Studies*. Ed. John Bryant. New York: Greenwood, 1986.

John D. Seelye, "Spontaneous Impress of Truth: Melville's Jack Chase: A Source, an Analogue, a Conjecture," *Nineteenth-Century Fiction*, March 1966.

Mitlon R. Stern, ed., Billy Budd, Sailor: *An Inside Narrative.* Indianapolis: Bobbs-Merrill, 1975.

Brook Thomas, "The Legal Fictions of Herman Melville and Lemuel Shaw," *Critical Inquiry*, September 1984.

Howard P. Vincent, ed., *Twentieth Century Interpretations of* Billy Budd. Englewood Cliffs, NJ: Prentice Hall, 1971.

E.L. Grant Watson, "Melville's Testament of Acceptance," *New England Quarterly*, vol. 6, 1933.

Phil Withim, "*Billy Budd*: Testament of Resistance," *Modern Language Quarterly*, vol. 20, 1959.

Jonathan Yoder, "Melville's Snake on the Cross: Justice for John Claggart and *Billy Budd*," *Christianity and Literature*, Winter 1994.

Karl E. Zink, "Herman Melville and the Forms—Irony and Social Criticism in *Billy Budd*," *Accent*, Summer 1952.

VIDEOS

Billy Budd. Directed and produced by Peter Ustinov. Based on the play by Louis O. Coxe and Robert H. Chapman. Anglo-Allied Productions, 1962.

The Curse of the Somers: *Billy Budd's Ghost Ship.* Directed by George Belcher. Narrated by Peter Coyote. Somers Documentary Film Project Limited Partnership, 1995.

OPERA

Billy Budd. Opera by Benjamin Britten. Libretto by E.M. Forster and Eric Crozier. Adapted from the story by Herman Melville, 1952. Directed for the stage by Tim Albery. A BBC—TV/RM Arts coproduction, 1988.

WEBSITE

American Studies at the University of Virginia: Billy Budd (http://xroads.virginia.edu). This site provides readers with an introduction to the work, a full text, and multiple resources, including allusions and nautical terminology.

INDEX